THE PEOPLE'S FAVOURITE POEMS

Published in Great Britain in 2018 by
Old Street Publishing Ltd
Sulivan Road, London SW6

www.oldstreetpublishing.co.uk

ISBN 978-1-910400-61-6

A CIP catalogue record for this title is available from
the British Library.

Typeset by JaM

Printed and bound by CPI Group (UK) Ltd, Croydon CR0 4YY

THE PEOPLE'S FAVOURITE POEMS

Out and about with Kipling, Larkin and the rest

GARY DEXTER

with illustrations by James Nunn

To Carole

THE PEOPLE'S
FAVOURITE
POEMS

CONTENTS

Introduction

In middle age, we feel the first intimations of mortality.

In my case, I developed an eye condition. This made the use of a computer impossible, which made my job as a writer and an illustrator impossible. My eyeballs ached and stung, and, to soothe them, I spent hours in Stygian blackness, achieved by forcing scarves and dishcloths into the tiniest chink in window or door. I could read books, but I had to ration myself to about ten minutes at a time. Tests revealed a degree of macular degeneration (the macula being the central area of the retina). There was also a history in my family of the eye condition known as Best disease, which leads to a loss of central vision. I went to various clinics, but results were inconclusive. Certainly no one could tell me why even glancing at a computer screen was painful. I began to think that there might be a psychosomatic component, but no one could confirm this either.

As I lay in my second or third bath of the day, light off and a towel over the bathroom window, I began going over some of the poems I knew, just to keep my spirits up. I'd always enjoyed poetry. I knew various scraps of Larkin, Blake, Dickinson, Poe, Shelley, and I thought often of the extraordinary words of Shelley: 'Poets are the unacknowledged legislators of the world.'

These words, as always, seemed more than a little absurd. Poets, running the show? Whether in the nine-teenth century or the twenty-first, poetry was surely a minority interest, an irrelevance in the lives of most people.

Or was it?

I manipulated the hot tap with my toe. Perhaps I could find out. Perhaps I could prove Shelley's maxim right or wrong. What if I stuffed my head with poetry to a ridiculous extent? Would anyone want to listen? Would anyone *pay* me to listen? How much of it could I remember?

I had a mortgage, I'd just got engaged to be married and neither my future wife nor I were gainfully employed. On top of that I had an undiagnosed eye problem. So what more rational thing to do than learn some Tennyson:

> Come, my friends,
> 'Tis not too late to seek a newer world
> Push off, and sitting well in order smite
> The sounding furrows...

I began cramming at the rate of a poem a day, aiming for 30 poems to start with. It took about a month. Some poems were short ('Infant Sorrow' by William Blake), some were long ('My Last Duchess' by Robert Browning), some were medium ('Bright Star' by Keats). The final 30 included Larkin, Eliot, Kipling, Shakespeare, Wordsworth, Rossetti, Yeats and a dozen or so others. Not an enormous number of individual poems, certainly, but spread carefully over all periods and styles, so that if I couldn't produce any individual poem, I could find a work-around: 'I don't know that particular poem by Betjeman, but there's another one by him you might like...' 'I don't know any poems by Leigh Hunt, but if you like the Romantics, how about this one by Coleridge...'

Then, one Friday evening in August, I took them out for a test run.

I remember the first time very well: my audience was a young couple, early twenties, smartly dressed, in a half-deserted pub. I gave them the spiel I had practised: 'Sorry to bother you, but, could I ask you, do you have a favourite poem or poet? The reason I ask –' hurrying ahead to give them time to think '– is that I'm a poetry performer, and if you have a poem you like, I can try to recite it for you from memory. And if you enjoy it – and *only* if' – with a flourish – 'I offer my hat at the end of the performance for any change you may have.'

They seemed doubtful. The young man said he only had credit cards on him. So did the young woman. (Only cards! Why hadn't I thought of that? Modern people, when they go out, are like Colonel Bat Guano from *Doctor Strangelove*. They don't carry loose change.) I prepared to retreat in ignominy. But then the young woman asked me: 'What's *your* favourite poem?' It seemed she wanted to talk. I told her I liked Eliot. She said she'd studied Eliot at university. The young man made interested noises. He didn't seem to know this fact. Then it struck me. They were on a first date. The immaculate clothes, the deserted pub ideal for talking, the fact that they didn't know anything about one another, the fact that they were eager to talk to me (conversation, perhaps, had been languishing). We started chatting about poetry, and the young man said that the only poem he knew was 'If—' by Rudyard Kipling, and he couldn't remember much of that. 'Would you like to hear it?' I asked, adding: 'It doesn't matter if you haven't got any money.' They were going to have a poem if it killed them. And so I squatted next to them rather uncomfortably, and told them how, if they could fill the unforgiving minute with sixty seconds worth of distance run, theirs would be the Earth, and everything that's in it, and what's more, they would be a Man, my son. I may have been blushing a little.

Then I left them to get on with their date.

The second encounter, with some Norwich supporters, was more financially successful. They were sitting outside the pub, and when I offered my wares, someone said 'Shakespeare'. I gave them Sonnet 18, 'Shall I compare thee to a summer's day?' They threw change onto the table: £1.50 altogether. (Not everyone carried plastic! Hooray!) 'Next time learn a poem about the Canaries.' I thanked them and departed. Walking up the road, I encountered a group of senior citizens outside a Thai restaurant. They asked for 'If—' again. I picked up £3. Then a run of rejections. Then, half an hour later, four or five pounds for 'Ozymandias' from a military-looking gentleman and his sister (or wife). The coins were accumulating. By 11:30pm my trouser-pockets had an inertia of their own. By the time I retired for the night – after about three and a half hours' work – I had made £50.

It turned out that people asked for the same poems

over and over again. 'If—' by Kipling, 'The Daffodils' by Wordsworth, 'Funeral Blues' by Auden. Most of the time they didn't know the title or the author. 'What's that one about "You'll be a man, my son".' 'Stop all the clocks.'

But there was another aspect to this poetry business, one that I had not anticipated. I would usually get no further than: 'Do you have a favourite poem or poet?' before receiving the reply: 'No', 'Sorry', or in the worst case: 'Fuck off'. If I got to the end of my introductory spiel it would be: 'Sorry, I haven't got any money' or 'I've only got cards'. I was learning about rejection, about being a temporary member of the tribe of beggars.

What does it mean, to be a beggar? Well, one asks, and asks, and asks; one asks so often, and is so often turned down, that one is progressively stripped of dignity. Dignity is the integrity of a person, their self-sufficiency, their lack of need. When one has dignity, one is an island cosmos. No one else's respect is needed; one respects oneself; one is therefore self-employed. Someone who begs exhibits the antithesis of this. A beggar says, 'I need.' 'I have failed.' 'Employ me in a parody of employment.' 'Help me with your money towards something better, so that I may be like you.' It doesn't take long for the beggar to begin to despise his donors, as the partners in this degradation. How could it be otherwise? And along with despising and being despised comes a sort of defiance, a swagger. The swagger goes like this: 'You think I am lower than you and our relationship is predicated on this, so I do not wish to disabuse you. And yet I am higher. I live on my wits.' Or in my case: 'You have heard the beautiful words that have just come out of my mouth. You are utterly cowed by them, and why wouldn't you be; I am cowed by them myself. And so I leave you, having relieved you of your cash which you worked for doing your silly job shuffling paper, you who will never know what it is to strip yourself deliberately of your dignity and thus plumb the depths etc. thank you goodnight.'

And then there was the sheer hatred of poetry itself. People (some people anyway) were violently allergic to it. They'd had bad experiences at school. They didn't understand it. It was pretentious bollocks. It was laughable embarrassing bollocks. It had nothing to offer in a world in which real things happened, such as death and babies and shagging. Never mind that these things were what poetry was about; it was about them in a way that occluded them. I should get out of their faces right now (or as one young man put it, with staring eyes and flaring nostrils: 'Go!').

My response to those who said 'I hate poetry' was often to say 'Yeah, so do I.' This puzzled them, and seemed strange even to me, and not a little masochistically ridiculous, but it was true. I could have called this book 'I Profoundly Sympathize with Anyone Who Hates Poetry' because sometimes I don't like poetry either. Poetry can induce disgust. Orwell, who at one time worked in a second-hand bookshop, said that books in large numbers are revolting. Meat is tasty, but the smell of a butcher's shop makes you feel sick. Particularly sick-making are the modern poets who seem convinced that they understand the wicked ways of the world and deliver their unrhyming, unmetrical poems in a sing-songy voice which is presumably supposed to suggest the passionate nervous prostration of a world-weary dreamer.

With an attitude like this I would never get an arts council grant. However, despite the hatreds and insecurities surrounding poetry, and despite all the rebuffs, snubs, brushoffs and damage to my *amour propre*, one in ten attempts resulted in a poem and a payment. Over the long run it came to about £12 per hour: better than the minimum wage. Poetry, it turns out, does seem to be important to some people. As with the other arts – theatre, painting, music – they will pay to experience it, to have it in their lives. Words, the right words, make people cry and laugh and fling their arms around you. Poetry makes sense of the biggest things: love and death, and occasionally both at once. Poetry is a memory of our grandmother; poetry reawakens hope in the desperate; poetry is a place of beauty that we can carry around inside us. Poetry is strong stuff: sometimes I wonder whether I'm really licensed to deal in it. I once recited Burns to a Scotsman (I am not Scottish) who, it turned out, had just been to a restaurant with his son to mark the one-year anniversary of the death of his wife; the reason he'd asked for Burns was because he'd had a Burns poem recited at his wedding. I felt utterly unqualified to have uttered the words. However, he *had* asked for it.

During my time on the streets, I was able to gain a reasonable idea of the most popular poems of our day.

The most recent poll to be published as a book was *The*

Nation's Favourite Poems, edited by Griff Rhys Jones in 1996. It was compiled as a result of a BBC Bookworm survey, from a rather limited respondent-base, i.e. self-identified poetry-lovers who listen to Radio 4. It is now very out of date. The number one poem in Griff's book is 'If' – which is, in my experience, correct – but number two is 'The Lady of Shallott' by Tennyson. This is quite laughable. Less than half a dozen people have ever asked me for 'The Lady of Shallott'. She's dead in the water. And several other entrants in Griff's top thirty are very rarely mentioned in the street. 'Abou Ben Adhem' by Leigh Hunt, 'Elegy Written in a Country Churchyard' by Thomas Gray, or 'Dover Beach' by Matthew Arnold. They all seem to have fallen off the poetic map. Either that, or most poetry-lovers are not listening to Radio 4.

Different ages like different poems. 'The Daffodils' is mentioned with a deer-in-the-headlights grin by people above 55. This age-group also ask for 'Journey of the Magi' by Eliot, 'Cargoes' by John Masefield and 'Adlestrop' by Edward Thomas. Ages 30-55 are more keen on Dylan Thomas (particularly 'Do Not Go Gentle into That Good Night'), Sylvia Plath and the Metaphysicals. The younger generation, whose poetic tastes have been quietly fermenting away since Griff's book was published 20 years ago, tend to favour Simon Armitage, Seamus Heaney, Wilfred Owen and (surprise!) Robert Browning, because these are among the poets who appear on GCSE syllabi. Young people also know about Spike Milligan, who seems to have hung on through sheer force of personality, as well as the new breed of performance poets such as Hollie McNish,

Harry Baker, George the Poet and Kate Tempest – though none of these appear in the top 30 and I don't personally learn their poems because Holly, Harry, George and Kate might take issue.

I have also found that younger people are generally more receptive to poetry than older people. In fact, young people are generally nicer, politer and more manipulable than older people. They stop and give you the time of day. Unfortunately they are also poorer: I remember one young woman and her boyfriend gravely giving me a very beautiful shiny two-pence piece after I had recited 'Jabberwocky'. The ideal client, if you can pin one down, is an older person who has just come out of an expensive restaurant, who has lots of cash (preferably in notes) about their person, and who is astounded that you can recite 'Leisure' by WH Davies.

Allowing for the fact that I have subtracted any still-extant poets, the book that follows presents the top 30 poems requested on the street, which I take to be the most popular poems of the day. They are different from the first 30 I learned; and in fact by the end of the year I felt it necessary to expand the database fivefold, in order to avoid embarrassment. But these are the poems that I end up reciting over and over again. I have devoted a chapter to each. Each poem is quoted in full, except in Chapters 7, 13 and 21, where the full poems were too long to print. The poems appear in order of popularity.

There are a couple of notable absences. No Ted Hughes in the top 30? No 'How Do I Love Thee, Let Me Count the Ways'? Only three women? Well, don't blame me. These are the unreconstructed demands of passers-by, and if I had to guess, I would say I've asked more women than men. These are the poems that people, encountered out shopping or drinking, actually ask for, and they are rhyming poems, many of them a hundred or more years old, by Kipling, Larkin, Owen, Dickinson, Wordsworth, Thomas, Poe, Blake and so on. All of them long dead. Something has gone wrong with modern poetry, and it's hard to know what, if anything, to suggest. Are schools to blame? Or the government? Rap music, TV, the internet? Ezra Pound? Or modern poets themselves? Are living poets writing poems that people want to read? Hard to say. Being neither a poet nor a historian, I feel less than qualified to judge. All I can do is report on the state of the nation. This is by no means all bad news, though, as we shall see.

So, please imagine the scene: it is 12:20am in Norwich. I have been bothering people for four hours, and I am tired. I am hoarse, my feet hurt, and more to the point, I am cold. It is February. There is a keen wind rifling up London Street. Oh, ladies of the night, in your glittering dresses and heels, with your bare February legs. It matters not how many of you there are. I approach you *en masse* and hold you with my glittering eye.

It's surprising how poetry changes people.

THE POET: Rudyard Kipling (1865-1936) was an English essayist, journalist, poet and novelist. He is best known for *The Jungle Book*, as well as for the most asked-for poem in the English language, 'If—'.

THE POEM: 'If—' appeared in the 1910 collection *Rewards and Fairies*, and is couched as advice to 'my son', who we may presume to be Kipling's only son, John. A melancholy tale is attached to John. He was rejected as unfit for the army during the First World War; Kipling, however, an ardent patriot, pulled strings to get John enlisted. John died at the Battle of Loos.

1

If—

BY RUDYARD KIPLING

If you can keep your head when all about you
    Are losing theirs and blaming it on you,
If you can trust yourself when all men doubt you,
    But make allowance for their doubting too;
If you can wait and not be tired by waiting,
    Or being lied about, don't deal in lies,
Or being hated, don't give way to hating,
    And yet don't look too good, nor talk too wise:

If you can dream – and not make dreams your master;
    If you can think – and not make thoughts your aim;
If you can meet with Triumph and Disaster
    And treat those two impostors just the same;
If you can bear to hear the truth you've spoken
    Twisted by knaves to make a trap for fools,
Or watch the things you gave your life to, broken,
    And stoop and build 'em up with worn-out tools:

If you can make one heap of all your winnings
    And risk it on one turn of pitch-and-toss,
And lose, and start again at your beginnings
    And never breathe a word about your loss;

IF—

If you can force your heart and nerve and sinew
  To serve your turn long after they are gone,
  And so hold on when there is nothing in you
  Except the Will which says to them: 'Hold on!'

If you can talk with crowds and keep your virtue,
  Or walk with Kings – nor lose the common touch,
If neither foes nor loving friends can hurt you,
  If all men count with you, but none too much;
If you can fill the unforgiving minute
  With sixty seconds' worth of distance run,
  Yours is the Earth and everything that's in it,
And – which is more – you'll be a Man, my son!

―•◦◉)

'If–' by Rudyard Kipling is the public's favourite poem. It consists of four verses of eight lines each, but there's no full stop anywhere in the thirty-two lines, making it a single sentence (depending on how you interpret the exclamation mark at the end of verse three).

'If–' is therefore one great outbreath.

It's not the easiest of poems to remember (I have often dried up in verses one and two), but it must be learned. It's the most popular poem, and a highly lucrative one. I've lost count of the five-pound notes or the cascades of coins that have followed its rendition. It touches people, it amazes them; and they are amazed, too, by my ability to perform it on demand, because it is not a short poem (neither is it too long to create in them a feeling of mild panic – 'When is

14

this guy ever going to shut up, and how much longer must I stand here with my face frozen into a rictus of appreciation?') It is just right, just long enough; and listeners, even if they can recall its actual words only dimly, have a sense of its shape, its duration, the inevitability of the slow winding towards its magnificent end, when the river empties out into the bay: 'You'll be a Man, my son.'

Sometimes I stop before those last six words and point to the person who has requested the poem. 'You'll be a Man, my son,' they say.

What is the appeal of 'If—'? I have seen men and women looking at me with something approaching rapture as I deliver it. Rapture, awe: they are transfixed, absorbed, transported, elevated.

This is an age of relativism. We've lost God and Manifest Destiny and gained Twitter and Google Maps. Here, though, is a poem that condenses an entire vanished moral and philosophical universe into about one minute – 'the unforgiving minute' that Kipling artfully deploys in the last verse to signify the arena of human activity, and which he makes, at the same time, the poem's approximate duration.

Not all philosophies are equal, and if Kipling's philosophy were bad philosophy, people would see through it and the poem wouldn't count for much. But it is not 'bad', not bad at all. It is Victorian. It represents a period when Britain was indisputably in the pink. They knew a thing or two, these Victorians, even if they were involved in some shady practices, grabbing diamonds and gold and adopting missionary positions. Let's cut the past a bit of slack. The poem deals with questions relevant to any age. How should one deal with unjust accusations? How should one respond to doubters? To lies? To hate? Is it possible to appear too wise? What is our right relation to our own ambitions? What is the role of pure reason in human affairs? How should one react to failure or success? What of the correct response to the destruction of one's entire life? How much should one complain about one's lot? What is the role of the will in general conduct? What about the effect of public adulation on one's self-image? Should one ever open oneself up entirely to another, even a loving friend?

These are some of the questions, and, unbelievably, they are not only asked, but answered, in the space of thirty-two lines. Someone from a past where there were no phones is able to speak to us right now and tell us exactly how to behave in order to inherit the earth and everything that's in it *and*, more to the point (infinitely more to the point) how to be a Man, with a capital M, something that in the early twenty-first century still eludes precise definition. Minor areas in the poem's extraordinary arc that might seem fleetingly problematic can be ignored or put aside for later as one surrenders oneself to this Man's Man, Kipling, not just a maker of exceedingly good cakes, who tells us how to live, how to heal our wounded and scarred lives. And women respond to this poem just as intensely as men; they are quite capable of making a small edit. It is all so simple! Just this: Be honest. Consider others. Don't get above yourself. Never give up. Don't complain. And you will be rewarded, a hundredfold, a thousandfold. No wonder people gape in astonishment. The daring of it! No wonder tears come to their eyes and they embrace you and surrender their money.

'How did you do that?'

'I work at it.'

'How many other poems do you know?'

'Well... I suppose a small book full. I try to go through about twenty-five each morning, just to stay on top of them.'

'Do you have a photographic memory?'

'No, not at all. My memory is just average. I work at it, you know. You could do it. Anyone could do it.'

'I couldn't.'

'You could.'

'Can we get a selfie?'

People have this poem written on their walls, even tattooed on their bodies. They credit it with inspiring their greatest achievements. But how closely, one wonders, have they really read it?

'If you can meet with Triumph and Disaster/And treat those two impostors just the same.' This aspiration is inscribed over the entrance to Central Court, Wimbledon. What can we take from it? That we should adopt the attitude of Shankara, the 9th-century Hindu mystic, who held that Brahman alone was real, and that the world was an illusion? That we should strive ceaselessly for our heart's desire, yes, but when we, after forcing 'our heart and nerve and sinew to serve our turn', get what we want, we should just shrug with a perfect indifference? Strange.

What about 'If you can make one heap of all your winnings/And risk it on one turn of pitch and toss/ And lose...' Sometimes when I get to this point I wonder whether my listeners will stop me in gales of laughter: 'You're having a laugh, incha?' We're supposed to dream and think and toil, and then when we've accumulated some of life's blessings, blow everything on one big punt? This is downright reckless. Never mind over the entrance to Central Court Wimbledon, they could write those two lines over the entrance to Paddy Power.

There is something curiously negative about 'If—', as if nothing is really worth anything, but we must pretend it is, just for form's sake. And it becomes truly disturbing when Kipling makes a foray into human relationships. 'If neither foes nor loving friends can hurt you/If all men count with you, but none too much.' It's all of a piece. The Old Kiplingtonian is invulnerable to those who love him and those who hate him, has put himself beyond being hurt, precisely because he is no longer attached to anything. This is quite inhuman. Humans are capable of being hurt precisely because they love. Why shouldn't another human being count for everything? Isn't it normal to experience unreasonable emotion? Do we really want to abolish the passions?

Which leads us rather to ask whether Kipling had been 'hurt' (his word) somehow. He wrote 'If—' in 1895 as a tribute to Leander Starr Jameson, the leader of the ill-fated Jameson Raid of that year: the Raid was an attempt to annexe the Transvaal for Britain (the Transvaal, controlled by the Boers, had lots and lots of lovely gold), an action which helped to bring about the Second Boer War. Was Kipling in love with Jameson? Who knows? Perhaps, by the time he wrote the poem in 1895, a member of Kipling's family had died or a business partner had betrayed him. Perhaps he had been beaten at school. It isn't really important: Kipling had almost certainly been hurt in some way, because we all have. But whatever had happened to wound him, he responded – in this poem at least, for Kipling was a multifaceted Man – by hunkering within himself in an act of self-preservation, giving his advice to the world to do likewise (I paraphrase): 'Withdraw: don't rejoice over your successes, don't grieve over your failures, keep a stiff upper lip, never love too much, never open yourself up too much – and if you do all this you will be given your reward, the Earth.' And what is this Earth? It all begins to look quite sinister. Is it the same Earth that Leander Starr Jameson and Cecil Rhodes (both of them Kipling's friends) sought to bestride like colossi, an Earth they hoped systematically to relieve of its diamonds and ivory, its emeralds and peacocks?

Is 'If –' Indian philosophy in the service of British kleptocracy?

THE POET: Philip Arthur Larkin (1922-85) was the author of four major poetry collections. In mid-career he sequestered himself in Hull, and had the reputation of being something of a recluse, but Alan Bennett once said that Larkin so enjoyed the acclaim that came to him that he became 'about as big a recluse as the late Bubbles Rothermere'.

THE POEM: 'This Be the Verse' contains in its title a nod to Robert Louis Stevenson's poem 'Requiem': 'This be the verse you grave for me/Here he lies where he longed to be'. It became Larkin's best-known work, and Larkin said that he fully expected to hear it recited by a thousand girl guides before he died.

2

This Be the Verse

BY PHILIP LARKIN

They fuck you up, your mum and dad.
　　They may not mean to, but they do.
They fill you with the faults they had
　　And add some extra, just for you.

But they were fucked up in their turn
　　By fools in old-style hats and coats,
Who half the time were soppy-stern
　　And half at one another's throats.

Man hands on misery to man.
　　It deepens like a coastal shelf.
Get out as early as you can,
　　And don't have any kids yourself.

This is Larkin's most famous poem, and the most famous poem in English after Kipling's 'If—'. Almost anyone can agree with its miserabilist agenda: children, because it allows them to feel, if only for a moment, that all their fucked-upness can be laid at the door of mum and dad;

and mum and dad too, because parents make mistakes by simply being parents – they can't help it and do not 'mean' it. In any case, parents are children too, and are thus doubly absolved.

Then there is that democratic 'fuck'. This has no business being in a poem. In the explosive, assonantal opening, 'you' don't only get fucked up, you get fucked up by your very own ma and pa. The title announces its high and separate status: 'This Be the Verse' (i.e. This Be the Verse and No Other). It's a poem that most people encounter outside the school gates, uncontaminated by any Department of Education imprimatur. The term 'parental advisory' might have been coined for it, since it's a warning about parents.

I recall one subtle evaluation of 'This Be the Verse' by a young man who I stopped with his girlfriend in Shoreditch. He later became a Facebook friend by the handle of 'Pinkus Mike'. He said: 'The first verse is just comedy. In the second verse you have to slow down at "soppy-stern". The poem gets more interesting.'

Indeed – by the end of the second verse the poem has suddenly changed. I think that the final two lines of the second verse –

Who half the time were soppy-stern
And half at one another's throats

– bear a resemblance to the final two lines (same metre) of Larkin's second-best-known poem, 'An Arundel Tomb':

> Our almost-instinct almost true
>   What will survive of us is love.

The maths slows us down to a crawl. 'Half the time' they were 'soppy-stern', or a quarter soppy and a quarter stern, though 'half the time' they were also 'half at one another's throats' (possibly, depending on how you read it), which gives each of those previous traits only an eighth, with the other two eighths of that half representing 'half at one another's throats' and 'half not at one another's throats', leaving a whole other half going begging – during which said parents might have been eminently reasonable. As for 'almost-instinct almost true', it keeps fading in and out of comprehensibility. We almost have this instinct (and therefore don't, finally), and this non-existent instinct is almost justified (but isn't, finally), so that

> What will survive of us is love

is finally demolished as an idea. Or is it? Difficult to tell.

And then, in the final stanza of 'This Be the Verse', there is the metaphor of the 'coastal shelf', the submarine strata of misery laid down by generations of well-meaning idiots. The poem has now journeyed a very long way from the fucking of the first half (you can't fuck underwater) and in its twelve lines has covered the distance from what is outrageous and funny to what is oceanic and brooding.

One other note: if we imagine Larkin chose this metre to mark his poem out as doggerel, we should recall that

some of the greatest poems in English have been brief
lyrics composed in iambic tetrameter quatrains (eight syl-
lables per line, four lines per verse): 'Vertue' by George
Herbert, 'Sweeney Erect' by TS Eliot or 'Loveliest of
Trees' by AE Housman, the last two of which are in the
Oxford Book of Twentieth-Century English Verse that Larkin
edited in 1972.

As it happens, I studied at Hull University when Larkin
was the librarian of the Brynmor Jones library there,
though I never really met him. The closest encounter I
had with him was when he told me to stop eating my
sandwiches in the reference section. I failed to make any
reply (I did of course put my sandwiches away): at the
time I revered him so greatly I could never have talked to
him anyway, and I now recite his most famous poem with
a sense of guilt and shame. Guilt because I use his poem
parasitically to earn money, and shame because I never
had the wit to talk to him as Andrew Motion did, bud-
dying up to him and writing his biography; no, the best I
could do was learn to regurgitate his poems.

'This Be the Verse,' as nation's number two favourite
poem, was to have a central place in my working life as a
poetry performer. I recited it to English teachers depressed
about the new curriculum; to bankers in Docklands; to a
boy smoking a moody roll-up outside a music venue who
said to me bitterly when I'd finished: 'Did you even under-
stand that poem?' (Very cutting.) I began to wonder how

much Larkin meant the poem to be taken seriously, if at all, since his relationship with his mother was extremely close right up to her death, and his relationship with his father, though more distant, was not especially problematic (though Sidney Larkin did take the young Philip on holiday to Nazi Germany). Perhaps the poem is more to do with not having children than with having parents, as in the last line: 'And don't have any kids yourself'. Larkin never did, and 'This Be the Verse' seems to have been his manifesto for not doing so. He may have feared that if he did have children he would fuck them up. The 'they' of the first line in this reading is Larkin's imagined 'I': 'I'd fuck you up, were I your dad.'

One of the first occasions I ever recited the poem was to traduce it. Around ten o'clock on a bosky summer evening I ran into a group of lads in Hawaiian shirts outside St Giles Church. There were about six of them, and they were all drunk.

'All right lads?' I said. 'I just wanted to ask you something. Do you have a favourite poem? The reason I ask is that if you do, I can try and recite it for you, and then if you enjoy it, I offer my hat for any change you have.'

'I can't remember any poems,' one said.

'Can I try your hat mate?' said another.

'I hate fucking poetry,' said another.

'Don't listen to him, he's pissed,' said yet another. 'He's been drunk since yesterday.'

This was Saturday night, so if he'd started on Friday, this could have been true.

'You can't remember any from school?' I said, a bit desperately.

'Listen,' said a tall beefy guy, getting up from a low wall and putting his arm on my shoulder in a way that could have been the prelude to anything. 'If you can put this word into a poem, I'll give you everything I've got.'

'Well, I don't make up poems,' I began.

'Listen, this is the word.' He came closer, his face in mine, breathing, serious. 'The word is shit. Faeces. Excrement. Any one of those.'

Panic. But then a realization: they were as pissed as farts, my brain operating-capacity was double their combined capacity at that moment, and I could have them right there – with the aid of Mr Philip Larkin.

'All right,' I said. 'How about this:

'They shit on you, your mum and dad.
    They may not mean to, but they do.
They fill you with the faults they had
    And add some extra, just for you.

'But they were shitted on in their turn
    By fools in old-style hats and coats,
Who half the time were soppy-stern
    And half at one another's throats.

'Man hands on misery to man.
    It deepens like a coastal shelf.

Get out as early as you can,
    And don't have any kids yourself.'

'Chyeesssss!' screamed one. 'That was fucking brilliant!'

'Not only that, it had some meaning too,' said the bloke who'd requested it, lucid through ten pints of Carling. 'Here you go.' And he emptied into my hat the entire contents of his pockets, amounting to about seven pounds in coins. The others too contributed. From that single encounter I made around £12.

— ❦ —

Anything as witty, mordant and popular as 'This Be the Verse' is bound to attract parodies, and during my time as a poetry performer I encountered a few home-grown ones: 'They buy you socks, your mum and dad', 'They tuck you up, your mum and dad'. The usual approach was to make the parody a bland celebration of parenthood, in maximal contrast to the original. My take, which I occasionally wheeled out, was as follows:

They feed the ducks, your mum and dad,
    They may not want to, but they do,
They figure it will make you glad
    To let you throw a crust or two.

It ends:

Man hands on kindliness to man,

THIS BE THE VERSE

It's fun if you aren't mean or dull.
Have lots of children if you can,
    And never go and live in Hull.

... which was heartfelt.

THE POET: Before the First World War, Wilfred Owen (1893-1918) was an English teacher at the Berlitz School of Languages in Bordeaux, and on the outbreak of war gave some thought to enlisting in the French army. He died on the 4th of November 1918, a week before the Armistice, having served in the British army since 1915.

THE POEM: By the time of this poem's composition in 1917-18, Owen was in grave doubt as to the morality of the war; during a period of recuperation away from the front, his friend Siegfried Sassoon said that he would 'stab him in the leg' if he returned. 'Dulce et decorum est pro patria mori' ('How sweet and honourable it is to die for one's country') is a quotation from Horace.

3

Dulce et Decorum Est

BY WILFRED OWEN

Bent double, like old beggars under sacks,
　Knock-kneed, coughing like hags, we cursed through
　sludge,
Till on the haunting flares we turned our backs,
　And towards our distant rest began to trudge.
Men marched asleep. Many had lost their boots,
　But limped on, blood-shod. All went lame,
　all blind;
Drunk with fatigue; deaf even to the hoots
　Of tired, outstripped five-nines that dropped
　behind.

Gas! Gas! Quick, boys! – An ecstasy of fumbling
　Fitting the clumsy helmets just in time,
But someone still was yelling out and stumbling
　And flound'ring like a man in fire or lime. –
Dim, through the misty panes and thick green light,
　As under a green sea, I saw him drowning.

In all my dreams before my helpless sight
　He plunges at me, guttering, choking, drowning.

If in some smothering dreams, you too could pace
  Behind the wagon that we flung him in,
And watch the white eyes writhing in his face,
  His hanging face, like a devil's sick of sin,
If you could hear, at every jolt, the blood
  Come gargling from the froth-corrupted lungs
Obscene as cancer, bitter as the cud
  Of vile, incurable sores on innocent tongues, –
My friend, you would not tell with such high zest
  To children ardent for some desperate glory,
The old Lie: Dulce et decorum est
  Pro patria mori.

The third most requested poem on the streets. And not too dissimilar from that other top war poem, with its indictment of the waste of war: 'The Charge of the Light Brigade'. In Wilfred Owen's war, someone had blundered, all right.

Owen's poem, like Tennyson's, is a poem for people who don't like poetry, who don't see the point of it. Recite 'Dulce et Decorum Est' and they suddenly do see the point, and thus (presumably) that if 'Dulce et Decorum Est' has a point, then perhaps other poems have a point too.

I have recited this poem to tittering teenagers, dour old men, open-mouthed lovers, a transvestite in high heels and a flak jacket, a girl with a poppy tattoo, and the brother of a soldier. I have recited it a hundred times and forgotten

GARY DEXTER

and flubbed it a dozen. I imagined I understood it. Now
I'm sure I don't.

It was a cold night (two degrees above zero) and I'd made
no money except from three girls who gave me 30p, the con-
tents of one girl's purse, for 'He Wishes for the Cloths of
Heaven' by Yeats. Then I met two youths in a deserted side-
street. Before I could even speak, one of them stretched out
a hand.

'Do you want this?' he asked.

It was an unopened can of beer. 'OK,' I said, and took
it, adding, 'What do you want for it?' I intended to offer
them a poem.

'Five pounds,' said the other one.

I laughed and said: 'I don't have that kind of money.'

He came much closer. He put his face into mine. He
had a tattoo on his neck, '1985'. 'Are you laughing at me?'
he asked.

'No,' I replied.

He repeated, still closer, his face lit with an intent to
harm: 'Are you laughing at me?'

On conflict and poetry, I thought I had a policy. At the
first sign of trouble, I would just walk away. And in the past
it hadn't been difficult to do, losing no self-respect in the
process. At the first sign of trouble I would just back off.
Because, as I told myself, if I wished to, I could get beaten
up five times a night. It wasn't worth getting involved,
especially with drunks.

I was wearing glasses and hadn't been in a fight for thirty
years. Looking in at the window of a nearby ladies clothing
shop I saw a bra and panties made of a beige fabric, and

33

thought what a strange colour it was. A sick feeling stirred in my gut. All of a sudden I felt 17 years old again, a time when skinheads were everywhere, many of them not very well-disposed towards me and my friends. I feared the first blow – where would it land? Knee in the groin followed by a kick in the head? So my policy went into action. I put both hands up – one holding the can of beer – and backed slowly away. Not ran, mind you: walked backwards slowly, looking at them.

Then the tattooed-neck one exploded with laughter. 'I was only messing with you,' he said.

The other one laughed too. 'He doesn't want any trouble,' he said, referring possibly to me, possibly to his friend.

They began to walk away from me, now, and I was left there holding the beer, my hands up, looking after them, my stomach churning.

'Sorry, mate,' the friend called back again. 'He's just got out of Hellesdon.'

They both laughed. What was Hellesdon? A prison? A lunatic asylum? (It's a lunatic asylum.)

What would Chuck Pahlahniuk have done?

In fact, what is poetry if you're not willing to fight for it? What does it mean to recite 'Dulce et Decorum Est' five times a night, a poem about men with blood gargling from froth-corrupted lungs, if you run away from a fight? I hadn't exactly run away, and it turned out that my adversary wasn't really spoiling for a fight after all; but I sensed that it would not have taken much – a push, a word in the wrong place – to turn a play-confrontation into a real one, with punches and kicks.

GARY DEXTER

The problem had its roots slightly further back in the conversation. 'What do you want for it?' I'd asked, and it was significant not because 1985 used this as a way of trying to find his way into a fight, or into mockery, but that I was attempting to use my own form of domination, or even belittlement: poetry. 1985 didn't know that, but it was true. Poetry, I have found, is a way of taming people, of bending them to my will: of impressing them, of aweing them, even. After all, I am using words carefully prepared and learned, the best words in the world. 'The best words in the best order.' Coleridge. Almost like weapons.

This is the problem. I am out there as an actor, dominating his audience. I am using, as every actor does, someone else's words to do it. When I finish reciting a poem, I bow. I say to myself that I bow to tell them it's over, but doesn't the bow imply ownership of the poem in some way? Can they fail to take it, obscurely, as some sort of ownership? After all, if I have remembered it and am able to recite it, I own it, don't I?

Is this the origin of the tawdriness I feel when I go out on the streets or appear on local TV? Not so much that I am a beggar at my age, but that I am living off the work of others? The Greats. Even, in some cases, still-surviving Greats whose work is still very much in copyright.

Wouldn't it be better to offer my own work? Well, then I would become one of those idiots who has learned his silly self-written lines and expects to be paid for them. I would not be what I am, someone who unexpectedly speaks the very syllables that someone carries within them, someone who produces the very page of the book read

35

and loved in childhood, the very page with its dreamlike illustration...

But back to 'Dulce et Decorum Est': I'm not sure if I really understand it. Bar a couple of flailing fist-fights at school, my experience of conflict is zero. If there were a war, I'd probably be a pacifist.

Owen, however, was not a pacifist: he was a fighter. Despite the impression he gives us, his war was not just about the pity and the victimhood. He and his friends were, after all, actively trying to kill Germans. The horrors that the Germans were inflicting on Owen, Owen was inflicting on them. Soldiers empty their revolvers into each other's faces, they bomb civilians, they grind children's skulls under their heels. These terrible acts lie behind this poem, and because of this, I have to confess I don't really know, first hand, what 'Dulce et Decorum Est' is actually about. If the idea that it's sweet and fitting to die for one's country is an 'old Lie', why was Owen involved? Is this a naïve question? Why wasn't he a conchie? That would have taken courage, if of a different kind.

I might understand a poem about civilians being gassed, because I can imagine myself in their place. But soldiers, who are both gassers and gassees? Who have decided that, in the scheme of things, they would rather defend their country, even if that means committing acts of brutality and harming the innocent, than bottle out? Not so easy.

─◦◉◦─

THE POET: William Wordsworth (1770-1850) lived a long life, playing the roles both of *enfant terrible* and Grand Old Man of English Verse, becoming Poet Laureate in 1843. With Samuel Taylor Coleridge he published *Lyrical Ballads* in 1798, marking the beginning of the Romantic movement in English.

THE POEM: It was inspired by a walk that he and his sister Dorothy took together in 1802, and was composed a couple of years later, after Wordsworth read Dorothy's journal entry for that day: 'I never saw daffodils so beautiful they grew among the mossy stones about and about them, some rested their heads upon these stones as on a pillow for weariness and the rest tossed and reeled and danced and seemed as if they verily laughed with the wind that blew upon them over the Lake, they looked so gay ever glancing ever changing.'

4

The Daffodils

BY WILLIAM WORDSWORTH

I wandered lonely as a cloud
   That floats on high o'er vales and hills,
When all at once I saw a crowd,
   A host, of golden daffodils;
Beside the lake, beneath the trees,
   Fluttering and dancing in the breeze.

Continuous as the stars that shine
   And twinkle on the Milky Way,
They stretched in never-ending line
   Along the margin of a bay:
Ten thousand saw I at a glance,
   Tossing their heads in sprightly dance.

The waves beside them danced; but they
   Out-did the sparkling waves in glee:
A poet could not but be gay,
   In such a jocund company:
I gazed – and gazed – but little thought
   What wealth the show to me had brought:

For oft, when on my couch I lie

THE DAFFODILS

In vacant or in pensive mood,
They flash upon that inward eye
Which is the bliss of solitude;
And then my heart with pleasure fills,
And dances with the daffodils.

—◦◦◉)—

Having spent the night in London, I was hitching up the M1, aiming to get to Sheffield. Hitch-hiking was my preferred method of travel when a student; but now, with the wisdom of age, I had hit upon a new method of cadging lifts: offering people a poetry recital. I would go up to them in the service station and ask whether they had a favourite poem – and if they had, and would like to hear it, whether they'd give me a lift to the next service station.

'Sorry, we're turning off before that at Junction 30.'

'Oh.'

Thus I had progressed from the Welcome Break at London Gateway, to the Moto at Toddington, to the Roadchef at Watford Gap, to the prettily-named Euro Garages at Markfield, finding myself at the Roadchef at Tibshelf, a few miles outside Nottingham.

The Roadchef at Tibshelf is an insult to the human spirit, but a good place to urinate.

Before accosting my next mark, I sat down with a coffee and perused a discarded edition of the *Nottingham Post*. Nottingham is of course the home of Byron and DH Lawrence. It seemed the muse had not deserted a recent *Post* correspondent:

Nottingham's the loveliest spot
   That ever could be found,
A castle, caves, two football teams,
   And Trent Bridge cricket ground.
There's cinemas and galleries
   And pubs to beat the band,
A skating rink, a concert hall
   Whatever you can stand.

Flinging this from me with a weak cry of revulsion, I saw some senior citizens debarking from a coach. I followed them into the Costa, and approached a group of about five women.

'Excuse me, ladies' – I never say 'ladies' in real life – 'could I ask you a question?'

I ran through my spiel.

'Sorry love, but I don't think there's any room. It's a coach party.'

'Oh yes, where are you off to?'

'The Abbeydale Industrial Hamlet.'

An industrial Hamlet. Some sort of theatrical robot?

'Give us a poem anyway,' they said.

'All right, what do you want?' I asked.

'What do you mean?'

'I'm a poetry performer. If you have a favourite poem I try to remember it and recite it for you.'

'I don't know any poems by heart.'

'You don't have to. I recite the poems.'

'Go on then.'

'No, you have to choose one.'

'Roses are red, violets are blue…' Cackles. But the speaker had seized up.

'Well, now *you're* reciting it,' I said.

'All right then, I've had a go, now it's your turn. Let's hear your favourite.'

'Let me put it this way,' I said patiently. 'I want you to suggest a poem.'

'I just did.'

'Not that one.'

'I'm rubbish at remembering poems.'

'You don't have to remember it. Just give me the title or the author and I'll do the rest.'

A species of resentment now set in. Just like being back at school, they were thinking.

'Daffodils!' said a bloke who'd joined the ladies with a couple of mates, and stood planted foursquare, hands in pockets, looking as if he'd just lost on a fruit machine.

'Very well,' I said.

I recited it.

Smiling faces. More than a dozen, now. Many laughing. 'Ten thousand saw I at a glance/Tossing their heads in sprightly dance.'

'That were lovely. Thanks love. That were great.'

'You're very welcome.'

'What's this all in aid of then?'

'I don't know, actually.'

Actually I didn't. No money, no lift. Some of them might have enjoyed it, but frankly, what was in it for me? Am I Wordsworth's lickspittle? I have no interest in educating the masses, even if I were able to. As soon as poetry starts being about improving people, it acquires lead boots and an iron cravat.

'Well, good luck with it.'

'Thanks.'

—◦◦◉◦—

'The Daffodils' or 'I Wandered Lonely as a Cloud' is one of Britain's best-loved and most-hated poems. Millions of English citizens, chiefly in the 50-80 age bracket, can name no other poem in the English language. Those daffodils *are* poetry: English verse stands or falls by them. I remember one woman chiding me for not reciting it in an expressive-enough manner. 'You've got to sway like you're a daffodil!' It may have been what a teacher had told her to do at school.

I personally grew to enjoy 'The Daffodils' as I settled into my role as a poetry performer. One reason is that it's a sweet poem about flowers; another is that if I hadn't enjoyed it I would have gone mad.

English people are supposed to know about flowers, or at least they used to be so supposed. In the film *The Wooden Horse*, one of the escapees from Stalag Luft 3, adrift in occupied France and covered in sand, throws himself on the mercy of the Resistance, but first the Frenchmen have to verify whether or not he really is English. They slap him to see what swear-words he uses ('What the devil?!' he exclaims, which passes muster) but the acid test is the following question: 'What flowers does your mother have in her garden?' He replies laconically: 'Lupins, gladioli, hollyhocks, nasturtiums...' Yes, he must be English. The English, they are crazy about the flowers. He is given money and chocolate.

Of course there's nothing wrong with flowers, but imagine the skewed perceptions of people who think that poetry is about skipping through daffodils like Fotherington-Thomas, and nothing else.

And if it's the only poem they can remember, they must have learnt it at school; and because they learnt it at school, the poem brings with it the frightful fear of humiliation, and the smell of ink and rugby socks, of metalwork shavings and burned butterfly cakes. And there I am, standing before them like their exhumed teacher, demanding they name me a poem. And so they produce 'The Daffodils', the only one they know, not because they like it or can remember any of it, but because they must get a good mark for English and keep their exercise book clean, and always draw a pencil margin on each page first, not just start each line an inch from the left side of the page, otherwise you *will* be penalised, and marked down a grade each time you do it. Is that clear? And there's nothing funny about the word penalised, it comes from the Latin *poenas*, meaning Carthaginian.

How distant we are from Wordsworth, and what a shame it all is. All right, 'The Daffodils' isn't the greatest poem in the world. But to have it represent the whole of Wordsworth! That's nothing short of a tragedy. Wordsworth is so much more. Those early years of Romanticism: what extraordinary hope and promise they breathe! What originality, so hard on the heels of Pope, Johnson, and

Swift! And the partnership with Coleridge, surely the most productive literary friendship of all time! The invention of the English landscape! Mind-altering drugs! Oh, their ridiculous youth! Tintern Abbey! *The Prelude*, my God, a 60,000-word poem-novel in which we see the philosophical underpinnings of 'The Daffodils' ('liberty' a significant word in the fervid years of fin-de-siècle Europe):

> With a heart
>   Joyous, nor scared at its own liberty,
> I look about; and should the chosen guide
>   Be nothing better than a wandering cloud,
> I cannot miss my way. I breathe again!
>   Trances of thought and mountings of the mind
> Come fast upon me: it is shaken off,
>   That burthen of my own unnatural self,
> The heavy weight of many a weary day
>   Not mine, and such as were not made for me.

A revolutionary, in his way, Wordsworth has been reduced to a sort of nervous floral spasm.

Should poetry be taught in schools at all?

THE POET: Robert Lee Frost (1874-1963) was an American poet whose work drew on his experiences of rural life, particularly in New England. His second-best-known poem is 'The Road Not Taken'.

THE POEM: 'Stopping by Woods on a Snowy Evening' was written in June 1922 at Frost's house in Vermont. He had been awake all night writing a long poem, and when morning came, went out to see the sun rise. At this point the idea for the poem came to him, as he later said, 'as if I'd had a hallucination', and he wrote it down within a couple of minutes. He called it 'my best bid for remembrance'.

5

Stopping by Woods on a Snowy Evening

BY ROBERT FROST

Whose woods these are I think I know.
   His house is in the village though;
He will not see me stopping here
   To watch his woods fill up with snow.

My little horse must think it queer
   To stop without a farmhouse near
Between the woods and frozen lake
   The darkest evening of the year.

He gives his harness bells a shake
   To ask if there is some mistake.
The only other sound's the sweep
   Of easy wind and downy flake.

The woods are lovely, dark and deep,
   But I have promises to keep,
And miles to go before I sleep,
   And miles to go before I sleep.

For those who don't know Sheffield, it's colossal, men-acing, crawling with enormous trams that look like they have blood on their consciences, and strewn with ancient factories with monster weeds growing out of their roofs. Glowering over the city is the Park Hill housing estate, built in the sixties in the Brutalist manner, and now half-deserted (as is much of the rest of Sheffield). The city is a place to respect mightily, to fear; and if you are born there, I imagine, to fiercely love.

I rarely get into arguments with strangers, but occasion-ally it happens. One such was on an allergenic summer afternoon in the beer garden of 'The Rutland Arms' in one of the most hideously magnificent graffiti-covered areas of Sheffield. I had just consumed a 'rutty butty' – a chip butty with melted cheese. The argument concerned the use of the word 'queer'. I was reciting 'Stopping by Woods on a Snowy Evening' by Robert Frost and itching.

'My little horse must think it queer/to stop without a farmhouse near' goes the beginning of the second verse of this poem. There is sometimes a suppressed smile at this point. On this occasion, though, there was outright laughter.

I stopped reciting. 'In the nineteen-forties,' I said, get-ting the date wrong, 'the word "queer" meant something different.'

'It sounds like he's getting queer with his horse.'

The speaker was a boy in his twenties, and for some rea-son I had already taken a dislike to him. It might have been because his friend – there were only two of them, sitting at a wooden table – was dickering with his phone and didn't seem at all interested in what I was saying; it might have been because this young man unsmilingly spat out 'Stopping by Woods on a Snowy Evening' when I asked him what he wanted; or it might have been because his shoes had an expensive look (hand-made?) and he appeared to have spent a great deal of time on his beard and general appearance. It also seemed possible that this comment about Robert Frost getting queer with his horse was meant for his phone-dickering friend, presumably to distance himself from the poem he had that moment chosen, because it contained the word 'queer' and he didn't want his friend to think that he might consider getting queer with *him*.

I now wanted nothing to do with either of them, so the recitation came to a halt. My watchword is respect for the poem.

'Do you want to hear the poem?' I asked.

'I'm not that fussed.'

'You agreed.'

'Yeah, but I'm not that fussed.'

I stood, tapping the table. Obviously now the recital was impossible. Who was this Frost with his little horse anyhow? Why couldn't he have had a bigger horse? Well, it doesn't scan: 'My big horse would think it queer.' 'Mister Big would think it queer.' 'Biggy-boy would think it queer.'

'I think you should respect the poem,' I said – not knowing really what else to say, but feeling this was the wrong thing – 'that you asked for.'

'I think you should fuck right off,' said the young man, not unreasonably.

His friend looked up. 'How about "It Was on the Good Ship Venus"?' he said.

'Fucking Good Ship Venus,' I said, and walked off, trembling a little.

Surprisingly there was no reaction from the two until I was some way away, and then unmistakably:

'Wanker!'

This business of 'queer' and 'gay' can be something of a barrier to communication. The words appear in the poems of Wordsworth, Thomas, Byron, Frost, Carroll, Browning, Poe. Wordsworth feels 'gay' when he sees daffodils:

A poet could not but be gay
In such a jocund company.

Dylan Thomas recommends his dad be gay at the moment of his expiration:

Grave men, near death, who see with blinding sight,
Blind eyes could blaze like meteors and be gay,
Rage, rage against the dying of the light.

Frost and his mare, as we know, are sunk in snow up to their knees and feeling queer. Then there are pussies: Edward Lear, that most unregenerate man, mentions pussies whenever he can:

O lovely pussy, O pussy my love
What a beautiful pussy you are.

(Twitter reaction as I performed this on Radio 2: 'I can't believe Jeremy's got this bloke to say "What a wonderful pussy you are" live on the radio.')

Should we lament the loss of these old meanings, and demand that they be reinstated? That would be like asking grown-up kids to come back to the teenage box-rooms they've left forever. We must let them go, let them change, let them pass – and anyway, as the old meanings have gone, new life has been given to them.

Nevertheless, does the fact that a poem includes words such as 'gay' and 'queer' prohibit us from entering imaginatively into its world?

I remember reciting Lear's 'The Owl and the Pussycat' to a group of girls in their early twenties, perhaps university students back home to meet old friends. They were done up with luminescent paint on their faces and clothes, and were carrying glow-wands. There were five or six of them. I had reinvented myself as a person who enjoyed approaching and chatting to attractive young strangers of the opposite sex, and after I had recited 'Jabberwocky', one of them asked for the Lear. So I gave it:

Pussy said to the owl, 'You elegant fowl,
How charmingly sweet you sing.
Oh, let us be married; too long have we tarried,
But what shall we do for a ring?'

... and there were no snickers, no smiles, nor did I smile at the mention of pussies: I wanted them to feel I *was* Edward Lear. I think we were all trying to be children, which may have been how Edward Lear felt. This is the magic of his poem, now perhaps more than ever: it allows us to repatriate ourselves to a Garden of Eden, or perhaps to a queer and lovely wood where the snow is falling.

THE POET: Dylan Thomas (1914-1953) was a hard-drinking, hard-womanizing, hard-versifying genius (a reputation he carefully crafted for himself), known for his play *Under Milk Wood* and a body of extraordinary poems including 'Fern Hill' and 'And Death Shall Have No Dominion'.

THE POEM: Written in 1947, it was published in 1951 in an Italian literary journal, *Botteghe Oscure*, edited by Marguerite Caetani, Princess di Bassiano, which published poetry in English, French, Italian, German and Spanish. The poem is probably the most famous villanelle in English.

6

Do Not Go Gentle into That Good Night

BY DYLAN THOMAS

Do not go gentle into that good night,
  Old age should burn and rave at close of day;
Rage, rage against the dying of the light.

Though wise men at their end know dark is right,
  Because their words had forked no lightning they
Do not go gentle into that good night.

Good men, the last wave by, crying how bright
  Their frail deeds might have danced in a green bay,
Rage, rage against the dying of the light.

Wild men who caught and sang the sun in flight,
  And learn, too late, they grieve it on its way,
Do not go gentle into that good night.

Grave men, near death, who see with blinding sight
  Blind eyes could blaze like meteors and be gay,
Rage, rage against the dying of the light.

And you, my father, there on the sad height,
   Curse, bless, me now with your fierce tears, I pray.
Do not go gentle into that good night.
   Rage, rage against the dying of the light.

This is probably the best-known example in English poetry of a villanelle (a verse form made up of five three-line verses plus one final four-line verse, with two lines that repeat alternately and are knitted back together in the final couplet). As with all villanelles, it exhibits Extreme Structure, but it nevertheless manages to sound very natural as a spoken poem, mainly, I think, because of the preponderance of monosyllabic words that we imagine we understand: night, burn, age, dark, end, sun, flight, sight, and, of course, gay (see the previous chapter).

The poem as a whole is not particularly easy to remember because the repeating final lines of each verse, all of which rhyme either 'night' or 'light', are easy to get mixed up. But once you have it committed to memory, it moves with an extraordinary inexorable quality, the final couplet having great emotional impact; the listener – subconsciously or not – realizing that everything so far has led up to this meeting and joining together.

Whenever someone in the street mentioned Dylan Thomas it would always be 'Do Not Go Gentle into That Good Night' that they wanted. Not 'Fern Hill' (thank God, because it is very long), not 'And Death Shall Have No Dominion', but this. There is no other Dylan Thomas poem in the top 50, in my experience. When the BBC book *The Nation's Favourite Poems*, a poll of Radio 4 listeners' favourites, came out in 1996, 'Fern Hill' featured at number 13 and 'Do Not Go Gentle' a long way behind at number 35. I would be willing to believe that my own sampling was at fault, were it not for the fact that 'Fern Hill' (a great and moving poem) was mentioned perhaps twice in the course of what must have been thousands of street encounters. Tastes have, therefore, changed.

'Do Not Go Gentle into That Good Night' was written in 1947, and is generally assumed to be about Thomas's dying father: 'And you, my father, there on the sad height'. Yet Thomas's father did not die until five years after the poem was written, at the end of 1952 (Thomas followed him less than a year later in 1953). One interpretation might be that Thomas was imagining the *future* death of his father. However, there is another interpretation, given the biographical facts. At the time of writing, Thomas's father was alive; Thomas himself was ill and alcoholic. Could this poem be read as a submerged meditation on the poet's own death?

> Wild men who caught and sang the sun in flight,
>   And learn, too late, they grieve it on its way,
> Do not go gentle into that good night.

One other thing that emerges from the odd time-lag is that it seems possible that Thomas's father, who taught English and was well aware of his son's work, read the poem, because it was published in a magazine in 1951. Writers do the strangest things. How would it feel to read a poem by your own child encouraging you not to go quietly when you hadn't even started to go; a poem which explored filial bereavement when the bereavement, your death, hadn't actually yet happened?

The ever-present temptation is to recite this poem as if you *are* Dylan Thomas. Nothing so crude as putting on a cod Welsh accent, but in the spirit and style of Thomas: orotund, slow, thrumming. This is a temptation I'm afraid I occasionally did not resist (again, I must add, not in a Welsh accent, which would have been truly immoral).

By the end of my year as a poetry performer I had memorized another Dylan Thomas poem for emergencies: it was 'In My Craft and Sullen Art', which is notable for dramatizing the very thing I came across over and over again: the fact that most people don't like or enjoy poetry. As the second verse puts it:

Not for the proud man apart
    From the raging moon I write
On these spindrift pages
    Nor for the towering dead
With their nightingales and psalms
    But for the lovers, their arms
Round the griefs of the ages,

Who pay no praise or wages
    Nor heed my craft or art.

That is, the very people the poet writes for, the lovers, those who deserve poetry to be addressed to them, are not interested in the poet's bleatings. Who would have thought it? Amazing! This was the precise attitude I encountered! A young gentleman with his arm around a young lady would tell me:

'I don't know anything about poetry.'

'You're talking to the wrong person, mate.'

'Do I look like I know anything about poetry?'

'What? You're joking.'

'I hate poetry.'

'I've always hated poetry.'

'Get a job.'

'Sorry, I've only got cards.'

'I've got nothing, look.'

'I don't carry change.'

'Reminds me of school.'

'Are you a teacher?'

'Poetry? I don't know any poems.'

'No, mate.'

'I haven't got any money.'

'Not interested.'

'No.'

'Ask her.'

'I haven't got a favourite poem.'

'Roses are red, violets are blue. Your poems are shit, and so are you.'

'My friend's a poet.'
'Sorry.'
'We're trying to have a conversation.'
'If I tell you a poem will you pay me?'
'Roses are red, violets are blue...'
'You want money for *that*?'
'Spit some grime.'
'Piss off.'
'Fuck off.'
'Go away.'

Vindication, in fact, of a great poem and a great insight.

THE POET: Edgar Allan Poe (1809-1849) was a pioneering American poet, short-story-writer, journalist, novelist and ghoul, who probably invented the detective story and pioneered our modern idea of the macabre.

THE POEM: 'The Raven' was published in 1845 and was inspired by the talking raven ('Grip') in *Barnaby Rudge* by Charles Dickens. Poe reviewed the novel for the papers and said that the raven should have served a more symbolic prophetic purpose. Immensely controlled and atmospheric, 'The Raven' contrives at points to read like a parody of itself, as does much of Poe's work.

7

The Raven

by Edgar Allan Poe

Once upon a midnight dreary, while I pondered, weak
and weary,
   Over many a quaint and curious volume of forgot-
   ten lore,
While I nodded, nearly napping, suddenly there came
a tapping,
   As of someone gently rapping, rapping at my cham-
   ber door.
"'Tis some visitor," I muttered, "tapping at my chamber
door –
   Only this, and nothing more."

Ah, distinctly I remember it was in the bleak December,
   And each separate dying ember wrought its ghost
   upon the floor.
Eagerly I wished the morrow; – vainly I had sought to
borrow
   From my books surcease of sorrow – sorrow for the
   lost Lenore –
For the rare and radiant maiden whom the angels name
Lenore –
   Nameless here for evermore.

And the silken sad uncertain rustling of each purple
curtain
    Thrilled me – filled me with fantastic terrors never
    felt before;
So that now, to still the beating of my heart, I stood
repeating,
    "'Tis some visitor entreating entrance at my chamber
    door –
Some late visitor entreating entrance at my chamber
door; –
    This it is, and nothing more."

Presently my soul grew stronger; hesitating then no
longer,
    "Sir," said I, "or Madam, truly your forgiveness I implore;
But the fact is I was napping, and so gently you came
rapping,
    And so faintly you came tapping, tapping at my
    chamber door,
That I scarce was sure I heard you" – here I opened wide
the door; –
    Darkness there, and nothing more...

Poe's reputation is still very much alive, particularly among
20-30 year-olds. Poe excites loyalty and pity: think of the
famous 1848 'Ultima Thule' daguerreotype portrait of
Poe, his face lopsided, his features weak and woeful, self-
knowing, ghastly.

Among Poe's supporters, he is credited with originating almost every modern literary genre. In tales such as 'The Masque of the Red Death' and 'The Pit and the Pendulum' he invented what we now call the horror story; in the 'Inspector Dupin' tales he pioneered the detective story; and he was certainly an important early practitioner of science fiction in stories such as 'The Unparalleled Adventure of One Hans Pfaal', which describes a journey to the moon (that 'One': Poe possessed an unsurpassed ear). Some people claim him as the true inventor of the modern short story itself, as well as its first true theorist. He was also an amateur scientist who, in his long essay 'Eureka', solved Olbers' paradox decades before anyone else (i.e. the mystery of why, if space is infinite, the stars do not shine so brightly as to make the sky white, since at the end of every line of sight there is a star).

He didn't actually invent poetry, but he was an extraordinary virtuoso in it, as witnessed in 'The Raven', a poem that brought him great fame while living. It is written in verses of five lines of trochaic octameter; that is, eight trochees (DA-dum), in verses of five lines followed by a trailing half-line. Except that the trochees are often not trochees. How to recite the opening two lines?

> Once upon a midnight dreary, while I pondered, weak and weary,
> > Over many a quaint and curious volume of forgotten lore...

It makes sense to make the first line trochaic, with stresses on 'once', 'pon, 'mid', 'drear', 'while', 'pon', weak', 'wear'.

But in the second line, if you do the same thing, you land on some syllables that would be unstressed in normal speech, and so dactyls (DUM-da-da) are called for: 'MA-ny a' and 'CU-ri-ous'. These are not, of course, inadvertencies by Poe. By acting as counterpoints to the main rhythm, the dactyls give life to the poem, relieving it of what might otherwise be a too-mechanical regularity.

As a narrative, 'The Raven' contains an odd inconsistency. It is this: the poem starts in the presumed distant-ish past ('Ah, distinctly I remember it was in the bleak December'), describing the unexpected visit of the Raven – but it ends in the present. The last verse is:

> And the Raven, never flitting, still is sitting, still is
> sitting
>> On the pallid bust of Pallas just above my chamber
>> door;
> And his eyes have all the seeming of a demon's that is
> dreaming,
>> And the lamp-light o'er him streaming throws his
>> shadow on the floor:
> And my soul from out that shadow that lies floating on
> the floor
>> Shall be lifted – nevermore!

Perhaps, to be generous, the Raven had kept him company all the time from that night in December to the moment of the poem's composition. But if this were the case, would the poet have to make the effort of recollection implicit in 'Ah, distinctly I remember', when the Raven was, at that moment, as he took fountain pen in hand, perched on the bust of Pallas Athene over his head?

—◦⊚◦—

I only ever learned the first four verses of the poem, which are in themselves fairly substantial. A recitation of just these 25 lines takes a good couple of minutes, which is long in street-poetry terms, or long enough. Put it this way: no one ever asked me to continue. And yet it was often much appreciated. I remember a self-assured and beautiful maiden, rather as I picture the lost Lenore herself, giving me a winning scratchcard worth £5 (she had already scratched it with lost and maidenly nail and knew it had won); and a young Welshman, perilously pissed, handing me a fiver with the thickly enunciated words: 'I've paid a lot more for a lot less entertainment than that.'

As mentioned, 'The Raven' (only the first four verses out of eighteen is quoted here) is about a Raven (capitalized) that visits a scholar late at night. By the repetitive croaking of the word 'Nevermore', the bird answers all the scholar's questions, chiefly commenting on the likelihood of him ever again seeing, in this life or the next, his beloved Lenore. Lenore is dead, and she has died young; she was 'that rare and radiant maiden', not 'that rare and radiant matron'. This is a motif in Poe: premature death. Poe's mother had died young, aged 24, in 1811 (as Poe's wife was to die, aged 24, in 1847). Noble Luke Usher and Harriet L'Estrange Usher, friends of Poe's family, after whom the short story 'The Fall of the House of Usher' was named, both died young, in 1814, in their twenties. (In the story, the twins Roderick and Madeline Usher, also die young, and their 'House' – their family line – is destroyed, the physical building dramatically collapsing into a mountain tarn at the end of the tale.) 'The Raven' reflects Poe's horror at something he knew well: the extinction of young life and the pain of being left behind.

Or, more specifically, the extinction of young female life. Poe said in his essay 'The Philosophy of Composition' (1846) that 'the death [...] of a beautiful woman is unquestionably the most poetical topic in the world.' And it is here that Poe can seem truly influential.

In the summer of 1841 New York was agog at the murder of Mary Cecilia Rogers, a sales-girl in a tobacco-shop. Mary was a minor celebrity, noted for her beauty and charm. She had been specifically engaged as a fascinating butterfly for gentlemen customers to flirt with; her shop was frequented by journalists and writers such as Washington Irving and James Fenimore Cooper. On the morning of Sunday, July 25, 1841, she left home and did not return. Three days later, her body was found floating in the Hudson, off Hoboken. She appeared to have been beaten, and a cord was wrapped around her neck. The murder was attributed to gang violence (there were reports that Mary had been gang-raped), but there were no compelling leads, and after several weeks of feverish speculation the case was dropped. Then Poe came forward. On June 4, 1842 he wrote to the Boston publisher George Roberts saying that he was going to 'enter into a very long and rigorous analysis' of the case in an attempt to solve it. His method would be 'altogether novel in literature,' since he was going to cast light on the murder through a fictional treatment of its details.

This tale was 'The Mystery of Marie Rogêt', and it was billed as 'the sequel to 'The Murders in the Rue Morgue'. It transposed the crime-scene from New York to Paris, and featured C. Auguste Dupin as the investigator. Mary Rogers became 'Marie Rogêt', and instead of a cigar sales-girl she became a perfume sales-girl. Her death by water took place in the Seine, not the Hudson. Otherwise the facts were the same. Poe introduced the tale with an almost audible licking of the lips:

> The atrocity of this murder, (for it was at once evident that murder had been committed), the youth and beauty of the victim, and, above all, her previous notoriety, conspired to produce intense excitement in the minds of the sensitive Parisians. I can call to mind no similar occurrence producing so general and so intense an effect.

Poe did not solve the case, but the story had a shaping effect. The particular variety of detective fiction that tends to dominate today is so-called 'crime fiction'. In the crime fiction of James Patterson, Val McDermid or Karin Slaughter, there is the same preoccupation with sexual violence and the brutal deaths of women. The corpses of once-beautiful females, in a lineal descent from Poe's Marie Rogêt or Lenore, are firmly settled in the mainstream. The morbolatrous, woman-haunted Poe reaches out to us from beyond the grave and continues to fashion our most delicious nightmares.

Which makes the loyalty and enthusiasm of twenty-something women for Poe rather interesting.

'I do love a bit of Poe.'

'That was wonderful, that was a moment.'

'Here, have a hug.'

THE POET: William Blake (1757-1827) was an English writer, nude sunbather, artist, Swedenborgian and mystic, best known for poems such as 'The Tyger' and 'Jerusalem'. He illustrated his poems himself, adding greatly to their suggestive power.

THE POEM: 'The Tyger' was published in 1794 in the collection *Songs of Experience*, a follow-up to his 1789 *Songs of Innocence*. 'The Tyger' is the companion piece to 'The Lamb' in the *Songs of Innocence*, and, while Blake's philosophy is complex, the poem appears to give equal validity to the demonic, creative-destructive aspect of the natural world and human existence.

8

The Tyger

BY WILLIAM BLAKE

Tyger! Tyger! burning bright
   In the forest of the night
What immortal hand or eye
   Could frame thy fearful symmetry?

In what distant deeps or skies
   Burnt the fire of thine eyes?
On what wings dare he aspire?
   What the hand dare seize the fire?

And what shoulder, and what art,
   Could twist the sinews of thy heart?
And when thy heart began to beat,
   What dread hand? and what dread feet?

What the hammer? what the chain?
   In what furnace was thy brain?
What the anvil? what dread grasp
   Dare its deadly terrors clasp?

When the stars threw down their spears,
   And watered heaven with their tears,

Did he smile his work to see?
    Did he who made the lamb make thee?

Tyger! Tyger! burning bright
    In the forests of the night,
What immortal hand or eye
Dare frame thy fearful symmetry?

How astonishing this poem is, even after a hundred recit-als. How much there is to discover in it. How quickly it departs from the simplicity of its opening, which might be suitable for a child's garden of verses, into something dark, complex and Promethean ('What the hand dare seize the fire?'), Luciferous ('On what wings dare he aspire?'). Who made the Tyger? Some anguished and suffering demiurge, perhaps, and if so, he made us too.

At around the half-way mark of my poetry year I got a write-up in a magazine, and following that, a local television interview. The first part of the TV segment was filmed in my own home, to establish who I was and how I had arrived at my private passion; the second part was filmed in the street, as I accosted members of the public.

Among those members that day was a young couple out shopping. They asked for 'Tyger, Tyger'. The woman was tall, slender and lip-ringed, with heavy black-framed glasses and a fringe cut high on her forehead in a manner that somehow gave her an intellectual air, a latter-day Dor-othy Parker; her boyfriend was shorter than her with the physique of a boxer, complete with broken and thickened nose, and shaven hairline so low that it seemed to terminate a few millimetres above his eyebrows. He turned out to be well-read, though in rather a perplexing way, because after the recital was over, he said:

'I see you went for the later version.'

'Later version?'

'Yeah, the original version didn't have the verse before the end. About the stars and the spears.'

(I checked this afterwards. All I can say is that the original lithograph featuring the handwritten text and painted tiger, which is the one Blake printed, reprinted and distributed, has the penultimate verse intact, and I have come across no evidence that there was any other version.)

The conversation having ground to a halt, the girlfriend broke the silence with a question:

'*Why?*'

'Why what?'

'Why are you doing this?'

Her question did have a certain weight. I had often wondered myself. To make money? Yes, but after six months it no longer felt easy; I should have been doing something more lucrative at my age; I should have been a lawyer by now. (I should have been considering early retirement from having *been* a lawyer by now.) Perhaps I was doing it to educate the public? No... in fact, definitely not; if I ever did any preaching, it was always to the converted.

'To see what comes up,' I said.

'And does anything come up?'

'No. Not really,' I admitted. 'I'm not much given to imagining there's a point to what I do. I just exist. It's something to do with the legacy of the 1980s.'

'What do you mean?' Eyes narrowing under Parker bangs.

'That's when I was in my twenties. Back then, we all thought we were going to die in a nuclear war.'

'Too right,' said a voice. It was a passer-by, a rangy man with horse teeth, late 40s, who looked like could have been a white Rasta, except for the fact that he was bald. He was carrying a little girl. I vaguely recognised him; this happened all the time, because I met dozens of people a day.

'The cold war was a total frigging nightmare,' he said. 'You didn't know if you were going to wake up dead.'

'Yes,' I said, glad of his support. 'It was a time of nihilism. So we dropped acid and smoked weed and so on.'

'And burgled petrol stations,' he added.

'And burgled petrol stations,' I said. 'There was nothing to be gained by working. There was nothing to be gained from thinking we had a future. We didn't.' The little girl looked at me interestedly. 'Requirement number one for a contented human being,' I said, 'the sense of a future, of a place, a time, where you will be able to achieve something. We didn't have that.'

'It was fun though,' said the bald Rasta, with a laugh.

'You may have had fun,' I said.

'I did. You got to have fun.'

'I've always needed alcohol,' I said, 'to have fun. Thus the poetry.'

'So you're doing the poetry,' said the boxer slowly, 'because of the threat of nuclear war.' He raised his eyebrows. They met his hairline.

'Yes,' I said. 'That is it, in fact.' I knew I would never again be able to give that as my reason for reciting poetry, but with the support of the ex-Rasta and his silently assenting child, it seemed a defensible position. 'Actually,' I continued, 'I still think we're going to die in a nuclear war. The world might be even be a more dangerous place now than it was then.'

Dorothy looked sceptical. 'Well, yeah, but there's no way anyone's going to start a nuclear war. It would be suicide.'

'Yeah, bu–ut,' put in the bald Rasta, 'Suicide happens. There might be some suicidal leader out there, some guy, you know, who wants to take the rest of us with him.'

'And who says it would ever actually be started deliberately?' I said. 'It could happen by accident.'

'Sounds like you want it to happen,' Dorothy said.

'Of course I don't want it to happen,' I said, a little put out. 'I don't want to die.' The film crew were fiddling with their equipment, the shoppers washed around us. 'It's just that... sometimes I think we're living in a parallel universe in which a nuclear war has not happened, when in all the other of millions of universes, it did.' I paused. Suddenly I regretted my words. The young couple, trusting in a logic that was obviously faulty, seemed entitled to that logic, for the preservation of their own sanity, their own sense of the future, and their own right to become lawyers. 'It's just a sense I have,' I said. 'I may be wrong. You shouldn't listen to me... I'm sure we'll all be fine.'

There is probably a technique in rhetoric – in fact I know there is, but I can't put a name to it – of establishing a truth by asserting its opposite: 'Brutus is an honourable man.' By which is meant Brutus is a bastard. But in my case I really had meant a sincere lie. It didn't work.

'No, you're not,' said Dorothy. '*I* think we'll be fine. You don't.'

'All right, I don't.' No point in dissembling, then. 'Humanity may be diseased. It may do some terrible harm to itself. And that reflects our creator, who was not the real thing himself but some second-string man. He didn't do a very good job. There's too much evil, too much suffering. "Did he smile his work to see?"'

'Blake,' said the bald Rasta.

THE POET: Wystan Hugh Auden (1907-1973) was acclaimed as a new voice in poetry while still in his early twenties, and published numerous collections of poetry as well as plays (the latter in collaboration with Christopher Isherwood). Joseph Brodsky called him 'the greatest mind of the twentieth century'.

THE POEM: 'Funeral Blues' is an elegy originally dedicated to a great leader and intended ironically; an examination of some of the trappings of the funeral makes this clear (public doves, sky-writing, muffled drums, etc). The last two stanzas, which are found only in the well-known final version, seem more personal.

9

Funeral Blues

BY WH AUDEN

Stop all the clocks, cut off the telephone,
  Prevent the dog from barking with a juicy bone,
Silence the pianos and with muffled drum
  Bring out the coffin, let the mourners come.

Let aeroplanes circle moaning overhead
  Scribbling on the sky the message 'He is Dead'.
Put crepe bows round the white necks of the public
doves,
  Let the traffic policemen wear black cotton gloves.

He was my North, my South, my East and West,
  My working week and my Sunday rest,
My noon, my midnight, my talk, my song;
  I thought that love would last forever: I was wrong.

The stars are not wanted now; put out every one,
  Pack up the moon and dismantle the sun,
Pour away the ocean and sweep up the wood;
  For nothing now can ever come to any good.

⤙๑⬦⤚

This poem is in a famous film, and is at Number 9 accordingly. As the film becomes less and less watched, it may fall back down the rankings and finally become as obscure as it ever was.

Auden gave it the title 'Funeral Blues', but it exists merely as number IX in the sequence 'Twelve Songs' in his *Collected Poems*. In fact there are two versions of the poem, the original 1936 version being satirical, referring to the death of a great leader, and the revised 1938 version being the one that is known today and recited at funerals.

As might be imagined, I have recited this many times. One of my favourites was to a young couple with a baby in a municipal park, who introduced themselves as 'from the notorious Chechnya': Zelem Khan (he; handsome and smartly dressed, looking like Chekhov with his neat goatee) and Nora (she; lovely in flowing white like Olga Knipper). Their baby was the apple of their eye, and together they were exiled for whatever reason in a know-nothing dump on England's eastern seaboard, spending time on a park bench, perhaps waiting for some culture to arrive.

Nora was very pleased to get her request, 'Stop all the Clocks'. I was unable to fulfil Zelem Khan's request for a Chechen poet I had not heard of, but he, coming from a country where poetry meant something, and where for hundreds of years the Russian Bear had periodically waddled south to gnaw on Chechen bones, was able to recite some of his hero's work for me. We then talked a little about the novel *Hadji Murat*, Tolstoy's story of fighting Chechens in the Caucasus, and Lermontov's *A Hero of Our Time*: blood, thistles, mountains, men with the noses of eagles, and other things not often encountered in a municipal park with a bandstand and toilets. Nora listened respectfully to two men talking about combat, one of whom at least had not been in a proper fight for thirty years.

It was one of those occasions where it seemed positively in bad taste to remind them that the original idea was to recite a poem for money, and so, when we had finished talking, I said my goodbyes and walked off empty-handed. However, Zelem Khan remembered, and came after me to press two pounds into my palm. (It was at moments like these that I had more than the usual sense of doubt about doing what it was I did – but, I tried to persuade myself, I was like everyone else, wasn't I, earning money for a service, like a baker or a banker. The alternative would be to be employed by the city council as a cultural ambassador, telling people they could have a poem free and then picking up a pay-cheque every month, subject to being inspected periodically by the authorities to see if I was meeting performance criteria: I would end my days like the girl in the Ronald Searle cartoon, who has spent her youth being chased by lust-maddened hearties and being voted Balliol College Queen of the May but who finds herself in middle age abandoned in some cubby-hole in the Ministry for Health with a poster on the wall saying 'Orange juice is good for you!')

And then there was another, less fondly remembered occasion. It was night, late, late at night, on a hill in Norwich in front of a row of closed shops, and I was with a paralytically drunk squaddie and his two friends. The squaddie, or perhaps ex-squaddie, was badly shaven and radiated aggression, and it made little sense to be anywhere near him, but he asked for 'that poem about stop the clocks'. Figuring that in the memorial mode violence was unlikely, I agreed.

'Yeah, but you've got to do it properly.'

This was irritating – like the woman telling me how to recite 'The Daffodils'.

'What do you mean?'

'My friend died in Afghan. His mate read this out at his funeral.'

'Oh.'

'You've got to put the same emotion into it.'

By Christ, by fucking Christ. 'I see. All right then.'

I began, trying neither to under- or over-play it (dissolving into sobs might look like parody, and in any case, how was I supposed to know how this mate had read it? Might it not have been the funeral itself, rather than the poem or its delivery, that was moving, and how was I supposed to replicate that?) I got to the last verse, but then made a slip. Instead of saying:

The stars are not wanted now; put out every one,
  Pack up the moon and dismantle the sun,
Pour away the ocean and sweep up the wood;
  For nothing now can ever come to any good.

I forgot the first line and tried to improvise:

Put away the stars; they are not wanted now

84

I said, but then found I had no rhyme for 'now' ('cow', 'how', sow'? 'Put away the horse, and put away the sow'?). Not knowing what else to do, I just went onto the last couplet, hoping that no one present would notice, though I buggered this up too, being a little rattled:

> Put away the sun, and sweep up the wood
>> For nothing now can come to any good.

I bowed. The squaddie's friends, a young man and a young woman, out on the piss with him but still comparatively sober, applauded, looking eagerly at him to join in. This was a very bad sign, the looking to him for approval, because they were obviously accustomed to seek his approval, probably because if anything happened without his approval, he was liable to go off at the deep end. In addition to this he was not applauding and his face expressed outraged contempt.

'That wasn't it!' he said.

'Yes it was.' It seemed important to deny everything. I think I also felt I could win an argument about WH Auden with someone as drunk as he was.

Then he did something very unusual: he put his hands in his pockets and pulled out all his money, and there was a lot of it, in change. And he flung it at my feet. Then stood glaring at me.

His friends immediately began apologizing for him. They ran around collecting the coins. 'He's all right,' they said. 'That was really good.'

I stood, preserving my poetic dignity. They gave me the money, which I pocketed. The squaddie and I continued to hold our ground, two people who knew that Auden had not been Got Right, one rightly aggrieved, the other ashamed. But the weight of all that booze was too much for him. Perhaps he did feel somewhere in himself that he couldn't win an argument about WH Auden. With a glower he staggered off.

THE POET: William Shakespeare or Shakspear or Shakspere (1564-1616) spent his career as a working playwright in London. His sonnets were not published in full until 1609, but were well enough known before then for Francis Meres to refer in 1598 to Shakespeare's 'sugred Sonnets among his private friends'.

THE POEM: The poet asks himself: 'Shall I compare thee to a summer's day?' No, he decides: that would be ill-advised, since a summer's day, in all its flaming windiness, would be an entirely inapposite comparison. He then proceeds to make said comparison.

10

Sonnet 18

BY WILLIAM SHAKESPEARE

Shall I compare thee to a summer's day?
  Thou art more lovely and more temperate:
Rough winds do shake the darling buds of May,
  And summer's lease hath all too short a date:
Sometime too hot the eye of heaven shines,
  And often is his gold complexion dimm'd;
And every fair from fair sometime declines,
  By chance, or nature's changing course, untrimm'd;
But thy eternal summer shall not fade
  Nor lose possession of that fair thou ow'st;
Nor shall Death brag thou wander'st in his shade,
  When in eternal lines to time thou grow'st;
So long as men can breathe or eyes can see,
  So long lives this, and this gives life to thee.

The Irish playwright, critic, polemicist, and activist George Bernard Shaw felt ambivalent on the subject of Shakespeare. In 1896 he wrote in *The Saturday Review*:

I pity the man who cannot enjoy Shakespear. He has

outlasted thousands of abler thinkers, and will outlast a thousand more.

And yet in the same article he also wrote:

> With the single exception of Homer, there is no eminent writer, not even Sir Walter Scott, whom I can despise so entirely as I despise Shakespear when I measure my mind against his. The intensity of my impatience with him occasionally reaches such a pitch, that it would positively be a relief to me to dig him up and throw stones at him, knowing as I do how incapable he and his worshippers are of understanding any less obvious form of indignity.

Shakespeare, as our national poet, is perpetually in the line of fire. Any hostility directed at poetry will always be directed at Shakespeare first, the arch-perpetrator of flowery foolishness droned by turgid teachers in close class-rooms on otherwise splendid summer afternoons. Those who hate poetry hate *him*. Those who love poetry, however, love him.

Sonnet 18 is of course the best-known and most popular of the sonnets. The next most popular is Sonnet 116 ('Let me not to the marriage of true minds') and then, quite a way behind, Sonnet 130 ('My mistress' eyes are nothing like the sun').

Sonnet 18 is about love and death: you, the love object, the poet says, will cheat death because I have immortalized you in verse. This is a) extremely confident, given that works of art can have a very rapid date of expiry, b) amazingly true, since this poem will almost certainly be read and admired for as long as civilization endures, and c) completely untrue, since whoever this is addressed to became a roiling mass of maggots almost before Shakespeare had put down his quill.

Spitalfields, the covered market near Liverpool St Station, is a good place to 'do' poetry: it's full of people strolling at a casual pace, willing to listen to unusual requests; and the stallholders don't seem to mind, as long as you don't approach people who are actively preparing to buy something. It is very polyglot: there you will find Italians at whom Dante can be recited (all Italians without exception know the first three lines of *L'Inferno* – try it – though they never know the next three lines, with which you can surprise them); French people (for whom I learned Baudelaire's 'Le Chat' and Rimbaud's 'Ma Bohème'– the only problem being that after you have delivered these in French they frequently wish to engage you in conversation in French); Germans, with whom you may try a little Brecht or Rilke ('Du musst das leben nicht verstehen', 'You must not understand this life', advice I try to stick to); Spaniards, among whom Neruda is popular, despite his being Chilean rather than Spanish (I learned two of his, one in Spanish, one English); and Japanese (I learned three poems in Japanese, two haikus and one longer poem).

On this occasion I had turned up at Spitalfields having forgotten my hat, and so had attempted to 'rent' one from a hat-vendor there: Mal, partner in 'The Last Stop for the Curious Vintage'. Mal refused to rent me a hat by the hour. However, after I had recited a poem to him – at his request – by ee cummings, 'If I have made, my lady, intricate,' ('I will know if you fuck it up', he said) *gave* me a hat, an act of very great generosity. The hat was priced at £20.

Meanwhile, three women, girls really, were looking at scarves in a desultory manner. 'Would you like to hear a poem?' I asked.

'I hate poetry,' said one. She was extraordinarily good-looking: about twenty-four, heavily and expensively made up, a mane of lustrous hair, an open coat made of some sort of luxurious white animal, silk blouse, 'thrust breasts' as Burgess would have termed them, smoking a cigarette through glossy lips. Cigarette-smoking is permitted in Spitalfields because although it is under cover, it is still technically outside.

'Why do you hate it?' I asked. 'Bad experience at school?'

'Actually we're English teachers,' she said, blowing smoke over me. She smiled. 'Now you're intimidated.'

'Not at all,' I said weakly. I personally was never sexually attracted to the teachers at school. 'How... I mean, why do you hate poetry?'

'Don't really hate it, as such,' she said. 'Just nice to have a break from it.'

'Well, I won't detain you then.' I looked at the other

two, hesitating. They were a little less dazzlingly superhuman. 'How about you two? Do you have a favourite poem?'

'What about that one by Larkin?' one of them asked.

'Which one?' Images of Mr Larkin, a three-woman man, pounding away on top of Monica, Betty or Maeve. 'I can do "Mr Bleaney", "The Trees", "Churchgoing", "High Windows", "Annus Mirabilis", or "This Be the Verse"...'

She named a title I could not only not recite but had never even heard of.

'Is that in one of the collections?' I asked.

'No, it's uncollected.'

Vindicated there, then – in a small way. What could it have been? 'Wanking at ten past three...'

'All right, Shakespeare,' snapped the first one.

'OK. The sonnets,' I said.

'Yes. Number...' – she exhaled all over me and I stepped to one side – '...one.'

'Sorry, I don't know number one.'

'Number... twenty-three.'

'No.'

'Number ninety-eight.'

'How does that go?'

'Number one hundred and eighty-seven.'

'There are only a hundred and fifty-four.'

'Well which ones,' she said grimly, 'do you know?'

'Number one hundred and sixteen? "Let me not to the marriage of true minds?"'

'No, I don't like that one.'

'Number one hundred and thirty?'

'What's that?'

'"My mistress' eyes".'

'Oh. No. I find that a bit... what does he say? "If hairs be wires, black wires grow upon thy head." No.' A nimbus of disdain.

'How about,' said the third one, who hitherto had not spoken, 'Shall I compare thee to a summer's day.'

'Very well,' I said.

Sonnet 18 is a gorgeous poem to recite if you are sure you won't stumble. I began, shamelessly taking the opportunity to gaze into number 3's eyes:

Shall I compare thee to a summer's day?
    Thou art more lovely, and more temperate.

She was more temperate than her friend, anyway. Reaching a conclusion:

So long as men can breathe or eyes can see,
    So long lives this, and this gives life to thee.

'It doesn't make any sense to say that to her,' said the first girl. 'Only the person it was originally addressed to will be rescued from death.'

'You're a literalist,' I said.

'Thank you,' said number 3, giving me a pound. 'That was very nice.'

THE POET: Spike Milligan (1918-2002) was an influential figure in British radio, television and theatre comedy, the co-creator of *The Goon Show*, the author of the play *The Bed-Sitting Room* (a post-apocalyptic comedy) and the novel *Puckoon*, as well as a series of serio-comic war diaries.

THE POEM: 'On the Ning Nang Nong' was written around 1959 and is among the most-commonly taught poems in British primary schools: other candidates are 'The Highwayman' by Alfred Noyes, 'Jabberwocky' by Lewis Carroll, 'The Owl and the Pussycat' by Edward Lear and 'From a Railway Carriage' by Robert Louis Stevenson.

11

On the Ning Nang Nong

BY SPIKE MILLIGAN

On the Ning Nang Nong
   Where the Cows go Bong!
And the monkeys all say Boo!
   There's a Nong Nang Ning
Where the trees go Ping!
   And the tea pots Jibber Jabber Joo.
On the Nong Ning Nang
   All the mice go Clang
And you just can't catch 'em when they do!
   So it's Ning Nang Nong!
Cows go Bong!
   Nong Nang Ning!
Trees go Ping!
   Nong Ning Nang!
The mice go Clang!
   What a noisy place to belong,
Is the Ning Nang Ning Nang Nong!!

This is the best-loved poem by Spike Milligan. Other favour-
ites are 'English Teeth', 'Silly Old Baboon' and others in the

collection *Silly Verse for Kids* of 1959. Teenagers can recite it; so can the middle-aged. It's so much loved, in fact, that it was voted the nation's favourite comic poem in a poll of 1998.

'On the Ning Nang Nong' was always requested during radio appearances. (As my poetry career wore on, I did several spots on Radios 2 and 5, among others. The idea was to take listeners' requests and then recite from memory, though this required an element of listener trust; it was radio, after all. At one point a photo of me in the studio wearing a blindfold was tweeted, but even this didn't really prove anything, since a blindfold can always be taken off. In fact, the only guarantee of authenticity was if I got a poem wrong or didn't know it, which happened frequently.)

'On the Ning Nang Nong' is not a very easy poem to remember:

> On the Ning Nang Nong
>   Where the Cows go Bong!

... is straightforward enough. However, on that Ning Nang Nong, there *is* a Nong Nang Ning – the first world, as it were, containing the second, a backwards world within a world, where the trees go 'Ping!' and possibly teacups fall upwards from the floor and reassemble themselves on the table. Then we learn that:

> On the Nong Ning Nang
>   All the mice go Clang

... i.e. 'Nong Nang Ning' has now become 'Nong Ning Nang.'

In my opinion, the key to delivering a nonsense poem is to take it seriously. It doesn't do to recite 'On the Ning Nang Nong' in a jaunty way – the words should be savoured and given weight. Having said that, I took to stopping completely at the word 'Ping!', and lengthening it out to mimic a life-support machine going flat.

Radio 2 never had me back. Radio 5 did, though, several times. 'On the Ning Nang Nong' is a sort of anti-poem, and it may have appealed particularly to the Radio 5 audience. Radio 5 audiences, it seems, are no-nonsense folk who like nonsense.

I remember one Radio 5 occasion. I was alone, utterly alone in the broom-cupboard/studio in Norwich, wearing headphones that pinched, doing the show 'down the line' to Salford. It was approaching midnight: the graveyard shift. Suddenly I found myself speaking to someone I knew. This was an uncomfortable experience, like being caught smoking in the street by your aunt. The caller was a retired gentleman who edited a free magazine, and who had the sort of incorrigible personality that one associates with door-to-door charity workers (or editors of free magazines):

'Hi Gary! It's David!'

'Hi David!' I said, at first simply assuming I was speaking to a random disinhibitee called David.

'Do you remember me?'

'Er...' I said.

'David! From the magazine!'

'Oh, yes!' I said. 'How are you?'

'Very well, thank you kind sir! Are you still drawing?'

'No...' I said. Should I ask Salford to put the show

on pause while I caught up with David? But this surely wouldn't work, given that it was live radio and everything.

'I'm still doing the magazine!' David said.

'Good!' I replied. Salford had gone to sleep. It was just me, David, and a seven-foot Pudsey for company. It was well past everybody's bedtime.

'What are you up to?' David asked.

'Nothing much,' I said. 'Just doing the poetry. That's why I'm on the radio.'

'Oh, right! Poetry eh? I phoned up when I heard you, to say hello.'

'Hello!'

'Hello! I was so surprised to hear you!'

'Yeah, me too! I mean, to hear you!'

'Yeah!'

'Not illustrating, then?'

'No, my eyes.'

'Oh. Well that wouldn't... that would... that wouldn't help, would it?'

'No...'

There was a pause. 'Well...' said David.

'Well, it was nice to hear from you,' I said.

'Nice to hear from you too! Keep it up!'

'Will do!'

Britain has produced many fine comic poets, particularly in the nineteenth century – Charles Calverley, Thomas Hood, Edward Lear, Lewis Carroll, WS Gilbert – and then, as the twentieth century turned, Hilaire Belloc, GK Chesterton, Edmund Clerihew Bentley, Stevie Smith, Pam Ayres, Roald Dahl, Wendy Cope, Brian Patten, John Cooper Clarke and Michael Rosen. It's possible that other nations have fine comic and nonsense traditions too, but if they have, these poems haven't travelled well – with the result that we don't tend to know about them.

What may be unique about the English poetic tradition is that because comic poetry is so respected and enjoyed, serious poets have often tried their hand at it. Here's Coleridge's brilliant squib on the story of Job:

Sly Beelzebub took all occasions
    To try Job's constancy and patience.
He took his honour, took his health;
    He took his children, took his wealth,
His servants, oxen, horses, cows –
    But cunning Satan did not take his spouse.

But Heaven, that brings out good from evil,
    And loves to disappoint the devil,
Had predetermined to restore
    Twofold all he had before;
His servants, horses, oxen, cows –
    Short-sighted devil, not to take his spouse!

William Thackeray contributed, among other efforts, 'The Lamentable Ballad of the Foundling of Shoreditch', a long poem that begins:

Come all ye Christian people, and listen to my tail,
    It is all about a doctor was travelling by the rail,
By the Heastern Counties' Railway (vich the shares I don't
desire),
    From Ixworth town in Suffolk, vich his name did not
    transpire.

Byron too had a go, as one might expect, with poems such as 'King George III Enters Heaven'; so did Leigh Hunt, Arthur Quiller-Couch, WE Henley (otherwise known for the magisterial 'Invictus'), Edith Sitwell and others. But it's when we go back to the eighteenth century that the penny drops. Jonathan Swift, Samuel Johnson, Alexander Pope were all, in their way, humorists, satirists, even if not out-and out comic poets. The well-spring of English poetry is humorous, and the existence of a Milligan or an Ayres in this context is not very surprising; only the gloomiest of serious poets could resist.

One who could, perhaps, resist, was William Wordsworth. And one of the greatest of all English comic poems, in my view, is about Wordsworth. It's by JK Stephens (a relative of Virginia Woolf who died young; Kipling called him 'that genius') and is entitled 'Sonnet':

Two voices are there: one is of the deep;
    It learns the storm-cloud's thunderous melody,
Now roars, now murmurs with the changing sea,
    Now bird-like pipes, now closes soft in sleep:
And one is of an old half-witted sheep

Which bleats articulate monotony,
And indicates that two and one are three,
   That grass is green, lakes damp, and mountains
   steep:
And, Wordsworth, both are thine: at certain times
   Forth from the heart of thy melodious rhymes,
The form and pressure of high thoughts will burst:
   At other times – good Lord! I'd rather be
Quite unacquainted with the ABC
   Than write such hopeless rubbish as thy worst.

THE POET: William Ernest Henley (1849-1903) suffered from tuberculosis of the bone from the age of twelve. Dauntless in character, he became one of the late nineteenth century's most prominent men of letters, and his followers were satirically referred to as 'the Henley Regatta'.

THE POEM: 'Invictus: The Unconquerable' derived directly from Henley's struggles with tuberculosis and the amputation of his foot. It was originally dedicated to his friend and patron Robert Thomas Hamilton Bruce. The poem has inspired many to endure: it was read by American prisoners in Vietnam. One prisoner, James Stockdale, recalled reading the last stanza of the poem written by another prisoner with rat droppings on a scrap of paper.

12

Invictus: The Unconquerable
BY W.E. HENLEY

Out of the night that covers me,
  Black as the pit from pole to pole,
I thank whatever gods may be
  For my unconquerable soul.

In the fell clutch of circumstance
  I have not winced nor cried aloud.
Under the bludgeonings of chance
  My head is bloody, but unbowed.

Beyond this place of wrath and tears
  Looms but the Horror of the shade,
And yet the menace of the years
  Finds, and shall find, me unafraid.

It matters not how strait the gate,
  How charged with punishments the scroll,
I am the master of my fate:
  I am the captain of my soul.

INVICTUS: THE UNCONQUERABLE

The story behind this poem is worth telling. Henley, the poet, had suffered from tuberculosis of the bone since childhood, and, in 1869, aged around twenty, was forced to have his leg amputated below the knee. Some time later he developed an infection in the other leg, and was told that this too, would have to come off. Henley sought a second opinion from the surgeon and antiseptic pioneer Joseph Lister, who undertook a series of operations to save the second leg, which were ultimately successful. It was during these gruelling trials that Henley wrote the poem.

Without knowing this story, there might be a suspicion that the poem is mere stiff-upper-lip Victorian bluster. In the context of its composition it is breathtaking. No wonder it inspired Mandela on Robben Island. No wonder there is an 'Invictus Games'.

What makes it all the more remarkable is that the poet does not avail himself of any theological panacea for his suffering; he does not entrust himself to the Deity; instead he takes a notably pagan approach to the hereafter: 'Beyond this place of wrath and tears/Looms but the Horror of the shade'. Even so, he is unafraid. The doctors could whittle him down limb by limb and his soul would be untouched.

As a twenty-first-century aesthete I don't find this at all convincing. There are many circumstances under which I feel sure that I would lose contact with my soul entirely; I can imagine myself buckling under pressure of amputation or battle or bereavement or just spilling hot coffee. Nevertheless – and I think this is why people respond so powerfully to this poem – I believe that Henley believed in his soul, and I stand in awe of his belief.

Henley is now known almost entirely for 'Invictus', but a look through the rest of his poetry turns up a mass of meditations in a similar vein, on love, mortality and death, the fleetingness of life and – very importantly for Henley – its ravishing beauty. There is much pagan mention of 'gods', as in this remarkable sonnet written in advance of one of the operations on his leg, 'Before':

Behold me waiting – waiting for the knife.
    A little while, and at a leap I storm
The thick, sweet mystery of chloroform,
    The drunken dark, the little death-in-life.
The gods are good to me: I have no wife,
    No innocent child, to think of as I near
The fateful minute; nothing all-too dear
    Unmans me for my bout of passive strife.
Yet am I tremulous and a trifle sick,
    And, face to face with chance, I shrink a little:
My hopes are strong, my will is something weak.
    Here comes the basket? Thank you. I am ready.
But, gentlemen my porters, life is brittle:
    You carry Cæsar and his fortunes – steady!

Henley knew almost every major literary figure of the latter half of the nineteenth century, and had a career as a poet, journalist and critic that some have compared to Samuel Johnson's in the century before. Henley was reportedly not unlike Johnson: massively-built, extraordinarily erudite, unfailingly witty. Robert Louis Stevenson took the idea of the peg-legged Long John Silver from Henley: it says a lot for Henley's even humour that Stevenson felt able to write him a letter cheerfully admitting it: 'I will now make a confession: it was the sight of your maimed strength and masterfulness that begot Long John Silver. Of course, he is not in any other quality or feature the least like you; but the idea of the maimed man, ruling and dreaded by the sound, was entirely taken from you.' Strange to refer to your own friend, to his face as it were, as 'maimed'.

But to get back to 'Invictus': the poem was not originally so titled. Originally it had no title, which would have made it difficult for it to become a well-known poem. It was simply number IV in a series called 'Echoes', and was only given the title 'Invictus: The Unconquerable' by Arthur Quiller-Couch, who included it as such in his *Oxford Book of English Verse* of 1902. He did Henley an extraordinary favour thereby: he granted him Posterity.

Immediately after 'Invictus' in the series 'Echoes' is number V, which is, in its way, as remarkable as 'Invictus'. This is one of the earliest experiments in free verse in English poetry, composed around 1875:

I am the Reaper.
   All things with heedful hook
Silent I gather.
   Pale roses touched with the spring,
Tall corn in summer,
   Fruits rich with autumn, and frail winter blossoms –
Reaping, still reaping –
   All things with heedful hook
Timely I gather.

I am the Sower.
   All the unbodied life
Runs through my seed-sheet.
   Atom with atom wed,
Each quickening the other,
   Fall through my hands, ever changing, still
   changeless
Ceaselessly sowing,
   Life, incorruptible life,
Flows from my seed-sheet.

Maker and breaker,
   I am the ebb and the flood,
Here and Hereafter.
   Sped through the tangle and coil
Of infinite nature,
   Viewless and soundless I fashion all being.
Taker and giver,
   I am the womb and the grave,
The Now and the Ever.

I had, in a minor way, my own health problems. Problems of vision, mainly. Hospital treatment had left me with eyeballs stained yellow; I fancied I was seeing yellow, as in a London fog of the nineteenth century. The stinging of blepharitis, the ache of the enlarged eyeball. (Be like Henley, man! Stop complaining!) And then, aching lungs, relics of pneumonia at eighteen years old (Henley had his leg cut off when he was twenty), freezing on the street in inadequate clothing, the occasional wooziness engendered by Benign Paroxysmal Positional Vertigo, tinnitus, inner ear eczema (Christ how it itches!), steroids and antibiotics, oesophageal reflux, extreme nervousness, blotches on the skin and neck, hysteria and ecstasy.

Two short girls, aged about sixteen, with sad faces. The first asks for 'Invictus'. It's twelve-thirty in the afternoon on a busy shopping street. 'Very well,' I say.

'But I need to go into Primark,' says the second and more doubtful of the two, perhaps wishing to withdraw from the contract.

'No problem, I'll go with you,' I say.

We walk together into Primark, its susurrus of Norfolk accents and clinks of clothing being unhooked, scrutinized and cast aside. The place is really a huge jumble sale. I begin reciting as the girls stop by a display of plastic jewellery:

> Out of the night that covers me
>> Black as the pit from pole to pole...

They are looking at the jewellery but also listening, especially the first. She has cropped black hair and seems, despite her youth, as if she might know something about 'the pit'. The air is full of perspiration and pushchairs and the smell of new Primark clothing being bought by people in old Primark clothing. I am dressed in Primark clothing myself. Henley was a cotton hospital-gown man.

> In the fell clutch of circumstance

I have not winced nor cried aloud.
Under the bludgeonings of chance
My head is bloody, but unbowed.

By the end of the second quatrain the recitation has attracted attention from a man in a shirt and tie with a name-tag saying 'Finn'.

Beyond this place of wrath and tears
Looms but the Horror of the shade...

'OK, could you take it outside, please,' says Finn, all cropped bristly neck and earwax, who perhaps objects to the loudness of my declamation (I had to be heard, after all, the place was noisy), and perhaps the insinuation that Primark was a place of wrath and tears beyond which only Dis loomed.

No matter that, apart from the first girl, I am being roundly ignored by *le tout Primarché*.

'Just a minute,' I said, 'It's nearly over.'

And yet the menace of the years
Finds, and shall find, me unafraid.

'I said *outside*. Come on.' Finn puts a hand on my shoulders. He is not looking at me, but straight ahead, towards the exit, or perhaps where reinforcements are stationed. Only that morning I had passed the benefits office and seen three security guards trying to restrain a man writhing on the floor who was repeatedly shouting: 'I'm going!'

Henley would not have gone, though, one foot off or not. And despite the fact that the girls are now looking embarrassed (worse in its way than frightened) I am fucked if Henley is going to be stopped.

It matters not how strait the gate,
　　How charged with punishments the scroll

'OK, Paul,' the man says into his radio.

'He's just reciting a poem,' says the second girl, surprising me with her support. The official pressure on my shoulder has now turned into a grip. I wrench myself away and walk to stand five paces off, next to some sunglasses with Union Jacks on the lenses. Henley would have approved. It is a good omen.

I am the master of my fate:
　　I am the captain of my soul.

I finish, bow, and then walk off quickly, my hands up. Paul is running toward me. I stride to the exit.

'I'm going!' I call out.

—❦—

THE POET: Thomas Stearns Eliot (1888-1965) was born in St Louis, Missouri, and lived for most of his life in England, having converted to Anglicanism (from Unitarianism) in 1927. Publisher, playwright, essayist and poet, he was the single most important force in poetic modernism, and liked cats.

THE POEM: 'Macavity the Mystery Cat' was one of the poems TS Eliot wrote for his godchildren; the poems were later collected in *Old Possum's Book of Practical Cats* (1939). The Times revealed in 2009 that Eliot also wrote a poem called 'Cows', aimed at the same audience. The cows in the poem do not come out very well; it appears Eliot disliked them.

13

Macavity, the Mystery Cat

BY TS ELIOT

Macavity's a Mystery Cat: he's called the Hidden Paw –
    For he's the master criminal who can defy the Law.
He's the bafflement of Scotland Yard, the Flying Squad's
despair:
    For when they reach the scene of crime – Macavity's
    not there!

Macavity, Macavity, there's no one like Macavity,
    He's broken every human law, he breaks the law of
    gravity.
His powers of levitation would make a fakir stare,
    And when you reach the scene of crime – Macavity's
    not there!
You may seek him in the basement, you may look up in
the air –
    But I tell you once and once again, Macavity's not there!

Macavity's a ginger cat, he's very tall and thin;
    You would know him if you saw him, for his eyes are
    sunken in.
His brow is deeply lined with thought, his head is highly
domed;

His coat is dusty from neglect, his whiskers are
uncombed.
He sways his head from side to side, with movements like
a snake;
And when you think he's half asleep, he's always
wide awake.

Macavity, Macavity, there's no one like Macavity,
For he's a fiend in feline shape, a monster of
depravity.
You may meet him in a by-street, you may see him in
the square –
But when a crime's discovered, then Macavity's not
there!

He's outwardly respectable. (They say he cheats at
cards.)
And his footprints are not found in any file of Scot-
land Yard's.
And when the larder's looted, or the jewel-case is
rifled,
Or when the milk is missing, or another Peke's been
stifled,
Or the greenhouse glass is broken, and the trellis past
repair –
Ay, there's the wonder of the thing! Macavity's not
there! ...

'Macavity, the Mystery Cat' is the best-known poem in
Eliot's children's collection *Old Possum's Book of Practical
Cats*, first published in 1939 (with a cover illustration by
Eliot himself) – which served as the basis for the musical
Cats in 1981, bankrolling Faber and Faber thereafter.

'Old Possum', of course, was Eliot himself. The name
was bestowed on him by Ezra Pound, and in return, Eliot
called Pound 'Ole Ez'. Both names derived from a private
game the two poets had, in which they would talk in 'Uncle
Remus' slang, Brer Possum being one of the Remus char-
acters. Pound's letters to Eliot are usually written in this
manner, even when discussing reviewers for Eliot's ultra-
lofty journal *The Criterion*. A typical example from Pound
to Eliot, dated 16 April 1938, reads:

> Waaal Possum, my fine ole Marse Supial: Thinking
> but passing over several pejorative but Possumble – oh
> quite possumbl – interpretations of selected passages
> in yr. ultimate communication, wot I sez appealin to
> you for the firm's interest, on your return from your
> Pasqual meddertashuns iz: For review copies of Kulch
> (to git it circd. despite mutilation of the title), Crite-
> rion better try H. Rackham, M.A., Christ's College,
> Cambridge (England), as he would know somfink
> about the las' chapter.

The letter ends with a pseudo-Remusian poem, which,
interestingly, mentions cats and possums in the same
breath but pre-dates *Old Possum's Book of Practical Cats* by
one year:

Sez the Maltese dawg to the Siam cat
  'Whaaar'z ole Parson Possum at?'
Sez the Siam cat to the Maltese dawg
  'Dahr he sets lak a bump-onna-log.'

It's notable that Eliot is the only poet with two poems in the top 30, the other being 'The Love Song of J Alfred Prufrock' – and both poems have cats in them.

At the Playhouse, in summer, it's nice to go into the garden. There's a breeze from the river, a pleasant shade from the many surrounding trees, and lots of tables, usually packed with people with no particular interest in the theatrical arts. It's just a nice venue. Many of them are smoking, which limits the opportunities for recitals (I have asthma) but most of them are out to have a good time, and this is a valuable commodity in the life of the – well, I nearly said *beggar*, but I should not claim that title. I am not homeless, I am not desperate, and I do not rely solely on handouts from the public to survive (though I'd be in Queer Street without them); I have not plumbed those depths; I cannot speak of them. Performer, then. Which makes the Playhouse a good place to work. Or so you might think.

A silent couple were sitting at one of the tables, and though the young man had an open tin of tobacco and some rizlas, he had not yet started smoking. The young woman was sitting with her hands between her thighs, bent over apologetically as if she were not used to going out at night and was afraid someone might accost her and ask her a question.

'Excuse me,' I asked her, 'I just wondered if you had a favourite poem.'

The young woman looked up with a jolt. She was about twenty-five and had long hair that somehow suggested it hadn't been cut since she was a girl. Her flowery dress too seemed childish and apologetic. Had they just had an argument?

'Oh, yes,' she said, timidly. 'Macavity the Mystery Cat.'

'Would you like to hear it?' I asked. 'The reason I ask is that I'm a poetry performer. I recite poems from memory.'

'Oh,' she said, with another jolt. But she wasn't looking at me – she was looking at her companion.

He, a backwoodsy fellow with drab clothing and a thatch of beard, running a little to fat, also about twenty-five, slowly began rolling his cigarette. Together they seemed like Amish lovers on a visit to the fleshpots. I hoped he would take his time about rolling the cigarette, because 'Macavity' is a long poem (the above is just an excerpt) and if he started smoking before I had finished, I would have to inhale his fumes.

'All right,' he said slowly. It was obviously up to him to decide. 'But I'm not giving you any money for it.'

'Why not?' I asked, disliking him.

'Why can't you do it just for the love of it?' he said. 'Why can't you do it because you want to, and not for the money?'

'I do want to do it. I promise you. I enjoy it.'

'You can't want to do it *and* want to get paid,' he said.

'No, I think I can.'

This was turning into a confrontation. Somehow I get myself into these fixes but lack the skill to get myself out of them.

'Would you do it without the money?' he asked. 'No, you wouldn't.'

'Listen,' I said. 'Where are you? You're in the Playhouse. Doesn't that mean anything to you?'

Standoff time. 'OK. I don't see why I should fucking pay,' he snarled, most un-Amishly, 'to listen to a poem.'

'Because actors get paid.' I said.

'Well, I'm not paying *you*.'

'Not everyone feels like that,' I said, walking away.

And that was the end of that.

As might be expected, I had a small stock of replies ready for people who were appalled that I might want to soil *poetry* with *money*.

Woman with feather boa: Why does it always have to be about money?

Me: Well, you do a job, don't you?

Woman with feather boa (cautiously): Yes...

Me: Does your boss ever come to you at the end of the week and say 'Why does it always have to be about money?'

A zinger, I'm sure you'll agree. But it didn't get me anywhere. Marking people's card never led to a donation. ('Omigod, you're right, you're so so right, here, have £70.')

But many did see the connection between poetry and

money, or, I should say, between a *performance* of poetry and money. There are people out there who like being *performed* to. They see its value, recognise the hours of practice necessary to be able to achieve a performance, and are appreciative. And one time in a thousand you come across someone who will step out of the shadows and be *very* appreciative.

It was a mild autumn evening, and, having donned my velvet waistcoat and trilby hat, thus magically transforming myself into an extrovert, I was ambling down St Benedict's in Norwich, a street of many restaurants. Outside one of them, I came across a tall, sandy-haired man and two young boys getting into a Rolls Royce. They were all three dressed smartly, the boys in spotless white suits. 'Good evening,' I said to the man. 'I don't know if you'd be interested, but I'm a poetry performer. If you have a poem you like, I'll try to remember and recite it for you.'

The man looked at me with amusement. 'I see.'

'And if you enjoy it, of course, and only if, I offer my hat for any contribution you might like to make.'

'A poem I like?' the man said. 'You mean any poem?'

'Yes,' I said. 'Within reason.'

'How about "Macavity, the Mystery Cat"?'

'With pleasure.'

'Boys!' he called into the car. 'Come out!' (The boys had already settled themselves in the interior of the Rolls; perhaps they were ordering drinks.) 'I want you to listen to this.' The boys were about eight and ten. They clambered out of the car and stood obediently on the pavement. Their hair was very nicely slicked. I paused, as if in thought, a trick I had developed that was, strictly speaking, unnecessary, and leaned down a little. 'Macavity's a Mystery Cat,' I began quietly, looking into their eyes. 'He's called the Hidden Paw. For he's the master criminal who can defy the Law.'

The information seemed new to them.

'He's the bafflement of Scotland Yard,' I went on. 'The Flying Squad's despair: for when they reach the scene of crime – Macavity's not there!'

The father and owner of the Rolls Royce: did he remember this poem from his childhood, and now, was I helping him pass it on to his children (if they were his children)? Was this occasion what it appeared to be? That is, a summoning of the past, with all the unknowable freight that pasts carry with them, as well as being – could it be? – the first time his children had ever heard this poem, felt its cadences, savoured the delicious non-appearance of – Macavity?

It's a fairly long poem, but not too long. I came to the conclusion.

Are nothing more than agents for the Cat who all the time
  Just controls their operations: the Napoleon of
  Crime!

I finished, and bowed. The boys clapped. They were well-balanced people who liked being performed to. The owner of the Rolls Royce took out his wallet, but then stopped.

'Do you think you could do one more?' he asked. 'There's someone who might appreciate your talent.'

'Of course, I'd be happy to,' I said.

'Just in the front,' he said.

I bent down and looked through the driver's side window. There in the front passenger seat was an old woman. I'd no idea she'd been there. I hadn't noticed her getting into the car with the boys. Had the father – her son? – come out a little ahead of his family and helped her into the seat?

The father opened the driver's side door and bent down to talk to her. 'Mum,' he said. There's a man here who can recite poems. Would you like to hear a poem?'

The woman didn't say anything.

'It's OK,' the man said. 'Get in, you can sit next to her. I'll go round and sit in the back.'

I got in, and, after a little hesitation, closed the door behind me, immediately cutting off all the noise from the street. It was very spacious, somewhat like a first-class seat on a train. White leather was much in evidence. The interior roof had a strange pattern on it – softly glowing stars. The woman was frail, eighty-five perhaps, and had carefully-curled hair.

The man meanwhile got in the back, behind his mother, and closed the door.

'Pleased to meet you,' I said to the woman.

She neither turned nor looked at me.

The man spoke from the seat immediately behind her. 'We're going to hear a poem,' he said.

She moved her head fractionally.

'I'm here to recite a poem for you,' I said. 'It can be any poem you like.'

Dead silence.

'It could be something you remember from school,' I said.

No response.

'Or anything that you particularly remember.' I paused. 'I'll try and remember it for you, and then I can recite...'

'Knocking on the moonlit door,' she said, cutting me off.

The relief was profound.

'Oh, that's one of my favourites,' I said. I wasn't lying. She was referring to 'The Listeners' by Walter de la Mare, written in about 1912. 'Would you like to hear it?'

No reply.

'I'll try,' I said. 'And if you don't like it, you can stop me. OK?'

No reply.

I licked my lips. 'Is there anybody there...' I began.

But I had only got to 'there' when the woman turned. '... said the traveller.' Her grey eyes were unclouded, and as she spoke the words I could almost sense her falling back through decades.

I gave her space to go on. She didn't, so I continued. 'Knocking on the moonlit door. While his horse in the silence champed the grasses, on the forest's ferny floor,' I said.

'Floor', she echoed.

'And a bird flew up out of the turret,' I recited.

Above the Traveller's head:
And he smote upon the door again a second time;
  'Is there anybody there?' he said.

The woman's lips moved a little as I recited, and when she looked at me there seemed to be a shadow of a smile on her lips, but it was dark in the star-glow-illumined interior of her son's car.

But only a host of phantom listeners
  That dwelt in the lone house then
Stood listening in the quiet of the moonlight
  To that voice from the world of men:
Stood thronging the faint moonbeams on the dark stair,
  That goes down to the empty hall,
Hearkening in an air stirred and shaken
  By the lonely Traveller's call.

I felt the car was no longer a car. It was a clearing in a dark forest. She was listening, but, in some weird sense, she was also, like the entities in the poem, a phantom, locked behind doors of time.

And he felt in his heart their strangeness,
  Their stillness answering his cry,
While his horse moved, cropping the dark turf,
  'Neath the starred and leafy sky...

I finished, and inclined my head in a brief bow. Then the

woman did something unexpected. She reached for my hand. I held it. Her eyelids fluttered weakly. No one spoke.

'Thank you,' the man said finally from the back seat. 'Did you enjoy that?'

'Thank you for listening,' I said to the woman. She let go of my hand. I got out of the car and stood on the pavement. The man got out too and came over. He extracted a fifty-pound note from his wallet, huge and red in the wash of light from the restaurant window.

'That was wonderful,' he said.

'Thank you,' I replied, accepting the note with some disbelief. 'That's very generous. I promise to spend it wisely.'

'Spend it however you like,' he said, putting his wallet away in his back pocket. 'You've earned it.'

—◦◉◦—

THE POET: WB Yeats (1865-1939) was born in Sandymount, Ireland, and is one of the most immediately recognisable and accomplished stylists of the twentieth century. He deals in his poetry with themes such as love, politics, myth and history.

THE POEM: It appeared in his third volume of poetry, *The Wind Among the Reeds* (1899). The person speaking is Aedh, one of Yeats' recurring poetic personae, who is permanently and incurably lovesick: the character of Aedh drew in part on Yeats' own experience of courting Maude Gonne, who refused several offers of marriage from him.

14

He Wishes for the Cloths of Heaven

BY WB YEATS

Had I the heavens' embroidered cloths,
   Enwrought with golden and silver light,
The blue and the dim and the dark cloths
   Of night and light and the half-light,
I would spread the cloths under your feet:
   But I, being poor, have only my dreams;
I have spread my dreams under your feet;
   Tread softly because you tread on my dreams.

And then, just up the street, perhaps the strangest encounter of the evening. A thirtyish man, handsome, soberly, fogeyishly dressed in woollen wear: practical for the weather, because this was now a damp winter night, but highly out of place; the local lads were in short-sleeved shirts, the girls in postage-stamp miniskirts.

His name was Peter. With him was a young woman; she had a soft face like someone's mother remembered from childhood, and curling gleaming hair; she had also a thick and sensible fawn coat. Laura. Peter and Laura.

After much wrangling with Peter, during which he was unable to name a single poem, a position I was inclined to regard as sheer cussedness (not unjustifiably given what came next) we finally settled on some Yeats.

> ...I have spread my dreams under your feet;
>   Tread softly because you tread on my dreams.

I came to a conclusion, gesturing at their feet.

'I didn't understand it,' he said bluntly.

'Well,' I replied, a little surprised, 'it's about the poet... It's a love poem. It's the figure of the poet, poor, in love, and unable to offer his beloved anything but himself, the clothes he stands up in, and his talent. It's the myth of the poet and the poetry of myth. The sun, the moon, the celestial orbs.'

'I learned poetry at school,' Peter said, who somehow didn't seem to be listening to a word I was saying, and had certainly not volunteered any money, 'but I never understood it.'

'Well, that is many people's experience. People say that all the time. I understand...'

'At school I didn't understand,' he cut in, 'the thing with the lines.'

'Lines? You mean rhythm?' I asked.

'No.'

'Metre?'

'No.'

'Metrical feet?'

'No. How the lines are divided up.'

'Rhyme scheme? AABB and so on?'

'No, I mean the way one line sounds the same as another and is repeated.'

'Alliteration? Assonance?'

'No. How there are, say, four lines next to each other.'

'Quatrain?'

'No.'

'Stanza?'

'Yes! Stanza. I never understood stanzas.'

This was an unusual complaint.

'It's just,' I said, 'that some poets like to order their ideas around a verse form.'

'Hold on,' said Peter. 'I'll give you a chance to show off, don't worry, but first can I read you some of my own poems?'

'*Some* of them? You mean, after all that, you're a poet?'

'Part-time.'

'All right... However, I don't really think of it as showing off. I should say that. I think of it as trying to earn a living.'

Laura stood watching. Why was this a leitmotif in my encounters? The man running the show, making a nuisance of himself, the woman patiently listening. Laura was so... passive. Her pale moon face.

'Sorry if I'm not saying anything,' she said. 'Actually I'm trying to digest a curry.'

'Oh, I see.'

'Can I ask you something?' she said. 'Do you really do this for a living?'

'It contributes to the household economy, yes.'

'OK,' Peter said. He was looking at his phone. 'Here's one.'

The first alteration
   Of the difficult situation
Of who and how I should be
   And how and why I should behave

... and so the long night wore on...

Was it my interpretation
   Of the fascination
That you hold
   Or was it the prospect
Of anal sex at twelve?

I laughed. 'Aha, I hadn't expected that. Very good. You deftly slipped anal sex in there. Nicely done. And the rhyme scheme. Quite Audenesque. And the subject matter too. Quite Audenesque.'

'You really liked it?' Eager.

'I did.'

The girl's face, suffering. The curry.

'Come and have a beer,' said Peter.

'That's a really nice offer, but I'm sort of working, although it doesn't look like it, I know. After I've done my quota, to be frank, I tend to want to go home and go to bed.'

'Come and have a beer.' There was something highly unusual about this young man.

'You're an interesting person,' I began. 'I'd like to talk to you....'

'Come on, it can be all about you, a monologue.'

Again, this *idée fixe* that I'm a narcissist, some sort of latter-day Swinburne – well, maybe not Swinburne – Swinburne must have been a very agreeable companion – some storybook self-absorbed poet, some vain child who only wants to talk about his trials and his sufferings and to bore the arses off people with his metaphors.

'I think I should tell you,' I said, 'I'm not interested in talking about myself. You've got a weird idea of me.'

'Come on. Come and have a beer.'

Laura did nothing to join in with his importunings.

'I'm really sorry,' I said, 'but I can't drink. As soon as I have even half a pint, my memory starts to go. I have to be completely sober.'

'Have an orange juice.'

'And the other thing is,' – struggling hard against his persistence – 'I have to earn another £15 this evening.'

'You can do that later.'

'Is he always like this?' I asked Laura.

'Yes,' she said immediately.

So we went for a drink. But I never earned the missing £15.

There were many occasions when I was asked to listen to people's poetry. These were often enjoyable, although somewhat tangential to my main purpose.

One was in London by the Serpentine. A few people

were sitting out on blankets, trying, through sheer force of will, to conjure summer. Among them was an older couple, in their forties, the woman maroon-haired, the man a little reminiscent of Will Self, with a prominent Adam's apple and a freelance air about him.

The woman asked for a poem I'd never heard of – neither the poem nor the poet – and as a result I was unable to oblige; but the man asked for something from Eliot's 'Four Quartets'. I responded with a well-known segment from the 'Burnt Norton' section, beginning:

Words move, music moves
    Only in time; but that which is only living
Can only die...

They listened graciously. Then the woman, pointing to the man, said: 'He's also a great poet.'
    'Oh, really?' I said. (A Great one, eh?)
    'Recite some of your own,' she told him.
    So he did. What was it about? Difficult to say:

And the calloused hand outstretched
    Holding the tip jar
I look at you over her bare shoulder
    Aware of how time digests the lives we had

And he knew it off by heart too.
    Or a young Welshman, who, after I recited 'Do Not Go Gentle into that Good Night', outside a pub in Brick Lane, surprised me with his own:

I saw the dawn's
  First flush emerge and tint the lawn
With colour like a boiled prawn
  After a night immersed in hardcore porn

—✎—

When I first went out on the street, I didn't know 'He Wishes for the Cloths of Heaven'. But then I had a rather spiky response from a woman who had requested it: 'Well, you'd better go off and learn it, then, hadn't you,' she said, making a little shooing motion with her hand.

So I did learn it, and found it came in very handy. Lots of people, I found, asked for it. And when couples who didn't know much about poetry asked me for a poem of my choice, I would bring Yeats out; and he was always very well received.

But I often wished I could meet the spiky woman again. There had been something unkind about the way she had dismissed me, something schoolmistressy; she had really seemed to take pleasure in telling me what to do and where to go. I wanted another chance. But of course, life doesn't work out like that.

Except that it does. Months later, I did meet her again. She was with a group of about a dozen people, walking down a little alleyway with shops, shuttered at midnight, and she recognised me.

'Oh, the little poetry man,' she said. (I am 5ft 11.)

Since meeting her I had had hundreds, thousands of encounters, but I recognised her: she was tall, slender, with long blonde hair, handsome, but also a little lost-looking. I felt now that her delight in telling me to go away sprang from something less than good inside her.

'How about some Yeats?' I asked, joining the group and falling into step with her.

'You learned it for me? You remember me?' she said, her eyes lighting up.

I am afraid a demon entered me. I wished to pay her back for the harm she had done me. I couldn't be generous. 'No,' I said.

The light died from her eyes. 'Oh...'

'Yes, all right,' I said, trying to make amends. 'I do recognise you. I recognise you. I learned it for you. Do you want to hear it?'

'If you like.'

I recited it.

... I have spread my dreams under your feet;
Tread softly because you tread on my dreams.

I finished. One of her friends shouted: 'That was very good!' But she said nothing, offered nothing. She walked on, ignoring me.

I had hurt her. The whole world felt sad.

THE POET: Percy Bysshe Shelley (1792-1822) was one of the central figures of English Romanticism, known for poems such as 'To a Skylark' and 'The Masque of Anarchy'. Vegetarian, feminist, atheist, he died young in a boating accident in Italy.

THE POEM: 'Ozymandias' was published in the 11 January 1818 issue of Leigh Hunt's *The Examiner*. At the time of its composition, the most recent hubristic tyrant to have risen and fallen was Napoleon, and the sonnet may contain echoes of the Romantic disappointment in Napoleon's career.

15

Ozymandias

BY PB SHELLEY

I met a traveller from an antique land
    Who said: two vast and trunkless legs of stone
Stand in the desert. Near them on the sand,
    Half sunk, a shattered visage lies, whose frown
And wrinkled lip and sneer of cold command
    Tell that its sculptor well those passions read
Which yet survive, stamped on these lifeless things,
    The hand that mocked them and the heart that fed;
And on the pedestal these words appear
    'My name is Ozymandias, king of kings:
Look on my works, ye mighty, and despair!'
    Nothing beside remains. Round the decay
Of that colossal wreck, boundless and bare
    The lone and level sands stretch far away.

Shelley wrote this poem after reading that the British Museum had acquired part of a colossal statue of Ramesses II. It was published in 1818, but the statue did not arrive at the museum until 1821, so Shelley could never have seen it there.

The statue is still in the museum. Hewn from gran-
ite, it is about nine feet high by six feet wide, and depicts
the head and upper torso of the pharaoh (not the legs).
It weighs around seven tons. Presumably, having survived
the last three thousand years, and now in an environment
protected from further mishap, it will survive essentially
for eternity, or as long as London is not hydrogen-bombed.

To put it another way, when Ramesses is obliterated,
Shelley will be obliterated. There may be human beings
who survive the cataclysm, on Antarctic Research stations
or deep in the Amazon rainforest (though even these will
have a hard job surviving the nuclear winter), but they
will have no interest in the charred remains of Shelley's
verse. Poetry of this sophistication, ultimately, is a luxury.
We will have urgent need of new stories, new myths, that
tell us what happened and why we came through it; some-
thing like the fragments of Christianity that live on, in
garbled form, in Russell Hoban's *Riddley Walker*.

This is not entirely irrelevant to the topic. Shelley
wrote the poem as part of a bargain. Around Christmas
1817 he and a friend, Horace Smith, both agreed to write
a sonnet on the theme of 'Ozymandias' (this being a
Greek name for Ramesses II), taking their cue from the
Greek historian Diodorus Siculus, who had quoted from
the inscription on a monumental Egyptian sculpture:
'King of Kings Ozymandias am I. If any want to know
how great I am and where I lie, let him outdo me in my
work.' Horace Smith's sonnet deserves to be remembered
alongside Shelley's:

GARY DEXTER

In Egypt's sandy silence, all alone,
    Stands a gigantic Leg, which far off throws
The only shadow that the Desert knows: –
    'I am great OZYMANDIAS,' saith the stone,
'The King of Kings; this mighty City shows
    The wonders of my hand.' – The City's gone, –
Nought but the Leg remaining to disclose
    The site of this forgotten Babylon.

We wonder, – and some Hunter may express
    Wonder like ours, when thro' the wilderness
Where London stood, holding the Wolf in chase,
    He meets some fragment huge, and stops to guess
What powerful but unrecorded race
    Once dwelt in that annihilated place.

Horace Smith, with great clarity and compression, does in his octave everything that Shelley does in his entire fourteen lines. And then, in the sestet, Smith goes further, pointing out the vulnerability of our *own* civilization. Just as a traveller might see the remnants of ancient Egypt and ponder on the transience of all human endeavour, so a future hunter may come upon a shattered London and wonder who built it.

Of the two, I prefer Shelley's version, of course; but I find Horace Smith's sonnet more ambitious, more prescient in this age of nuclear weapons, and more chilling.

Camden Market. I was there with Adonia Afroudakis, who was taking pictures of me for the *Sunday Telegraph*, to appear in the slot 'A Day in the Life'. Adonia was from Kefalonia, Greece, and wished to return there, despite 70% of her friends being unemployed. Her father lived in Nagano, Japan, a city I have visited. It occurred to me that her father could be younger than me. The thought was mildly horrifying.

Adonia was 21, and had a scar on her chin which I wanted to ask her about. She took photos of me posing by Victorian brick and railings, holding a straw hat in my hand, gazing poetically upwards (O for a muse of fire!).

We walked around the market chatting and looking for people to approach so she could get 'reaction shots' to my recitations.

A burly young man listened to my poem 'Mustard in Your Hair', then said he didn't understand it and asked why I'd chosen mustard. He promised me some change, but first had to go into a café to get some. Adonia and I waited for a few minutes but he didn't reappear. I thought: why am I, 54 years old, waiting for him to come out and give me a pound for a poem he didn't like? It's demeaning. We walked off.

We encountered five French guys for whom I recited Rimbaud's 'Ma Bohème'. They listened politely and then started a discussion about whether 'elastic' could have existed in 1885 (the poem mentions 'les élastiques de mes souliers blessés'). It seemed a particularly French conversation. We finally agreed that the word 'elastic' could have been a word for shoelaces that was later used for the stretchy fabric when it was invented.

I declaimed the first three lines of Dante's *Inferno* for an old Italian couple. 'Bravo,' the old man said.

A Tanzanian man and Japanese woman listened while I recited Tōson Shimazaki's short poem 'Furusatō' ('Hometown'). (In 2014 I went to Tōson's hometown, Magome, which, coincidentally, is just south of Nagano, and which was overrun with tourists, including myself.)

Then an encounter with two guys who looked like they wouldn't turn down a strange request – and didn't. To be more precise, they looked like they would engage with a stranger even if only to take the piss. Both men were short and beady of eye, and one was wearing a leather trilby. The trilby-wearer was very ugly, like the painting of the Duchess by Quentin Matsys; and, like the Duchess, he was not letting the fact bother him.

'A poem?' he said in response to my request. He pondered. 'I don't know any poems,' he said finally. 'No hold on, wait a minute, what's that one about daffodils.'

'No, no,' said the other. He was younger and chubbier. 'Ozymandias.'

'Ozymandias by Shelley?' I asked.

The trilby-wearer turned to Adonia. 'What do you do, do you recite poems too?'

'No, I take pictures.'

'What's this in aid of?'

'It's for the *Sunday Telegraph*.'

'Does that mean I'll be in the paper?' the trilby-wearer asked.

'It should be in this Sunday,' Adonia said.

'How about you take a picture of me and her?' he asked

me. 'Here, give me the camera.' He reached for it but Adonia took a step back. 'You're all right love, I was only kidding.'

'How about that poem, then,' I said.

'All right, but what's it you said? What's it about?' asked the trilby-wearer.

'It's about a traveller who comes across a statue in the desert. The statue is all broken, and on the pedestal he reads that it once... er... depicted the king Ozymandias.'

'Ozywhat?'

'Mandias.'

'What sort of a name's that?'

'Well, I think it's Greek, actually,' I said. Turning to Adonia: 'Isn't it?'

Adonia shrugged.

'You Greek then?' the trilby-wearer asked her.

'Yes.'

'Where you from?'

'Kefalonia.'

'Kefalonia, where's that then.'

'It's an island in the west.'

'Do you do poems?'

'No, I take pictures.'

'Go on, then. Have one of me.' A pose.

'Shall I recite the poem?' I asked.

'What do you want for it?'

'It's free,' I said.

'I don't like the sound of that. What's the catch?'

'OK,' I said, losing the will to continue. 'Let's leave it, then.' I gestured to Adonia to go.

'Hold on, hold on,' said the trilby-wearer. 'I didn't say I didn't want to hear it. I've got one for you though.'

'No, it's OK,' I said as we walked off. How strange: the roles were reversed. It wasn't entirely pleasant.

'No, hold on, hold on.' The man was actually coming after us. '"There was a young lady from Ealing..."'

We were walking away from him now.

'"Who had a peculiar feeling. She lay on her back, and opened her crack, and pissed all over the ceiling."'

We were now about ten paces away. 'How about that one?' he shouted. 'Hold on, hold on!'

We rounded a corner, then another. It's easy to throw off pursuers in Camden Market.

THE POET: Alfred Tennyson, Poet Laureate after Wordsworth, and author of 'Maud', 'The Idylls of the King', and 'In Memoriam AHH', is the quintessential poet of the Victorian era. Bertrand Russell called him 'an appalling exhibitionist' and suspected him of using make-up.

THE POEM: It was written in 1854 shortly after reading a newspaper report of the charge during the Battle of Balaclava. Tennyson made a wax cylinder recording of the poem in 1890. There is also a little-known companion piece, 'The Charge of the Heavy Brigade'.

16

The Charge of the Light Brigade

BY ALFRED, LORD TENNYSON

I
Half a league, half a league,
  Half a league onward,
All in the valley of Death
  Rode the six hundred.
'Forward, the Light Brigade!
  Charge for the guns!' he said.
Into the valley of Death
  Rode the six hundred.

II
'Forward, the Light Brigade!'
  Was there a man dismayed?
Not though the soldier knew
  Someone had blundered.
Theirs not to make reply,
  Theirs not to reason why,
Theirs but to do and die.
  Into the valley of Death
Rode the six hundred.

THE CHARGE OF THE LIGHT BRIGADE

III

Cannon to right of them,
  Cannon to left of them,
Cannon in front of them
  Volleyed and thundered;
Stormed at with shot and shell,
  Boldly they rode and well,
Into the jaws of Death,
  Into the mouth of hell
Rode the six hundred.

IV

Flashed all their sabres bare,
  Flashed as they turned in air
Sabring the gunners there,
  Charging an army, while
All the world wondered.
  Plunged in the battery-smoke
Right through the line they broke;
  Cossack and Russian
Reeled from the sabre stroke
  Shattered and sundered.
Then they rode back, but not
  Not the six hundred.

V

Cannon to right of them,
  Cannon to left of them,
Cannon behind them
  Volleyed and thundered;

Stormed at with shot and shell,
　While horse and hero fell.
They that had fought so well
　Came through the jaws of Death,
Back from the mouth of hell,
　All that was left of them,
Left of six hundred.

VI
When can their glory fade?
　O the wild charge they made!
All the world wondered.
　Honour the charge they made!
Honour the Light Brigade,
　Noble six hundred!

———✦———

In bed when the phone rings: I answer it in my underwear. It's Radio 5, and it's 'Poetry Day' at ten to eight in the morning. They want to hear what I have to say about poetry, and there are some grime artists on. I can do the interview live over the phone, and it will start in ten minutes.

Frenzied search for tea and clothing. Wondering why I am doing this. 'Poetry enables us to think about the deepest experiences of our lives.' No time for an evacuation. 'When others say: "No words could express…", poets say: "I can express…", and do.' Grime artists. I have my opinions: my opinions are that I respect them but I suspect that their lyrics would die on paper. (I can't understand the lyrics so

I don't actually know if this is true.) Emily Dickinson, on the other hand, lives forever. Better not broach.

They ring back. 'You're live after the news,' the studio woman says.

My mouth is dry. They will ask for literally any poem that exists. Why do I do this? It's madness. Of course, I could cheat. I have a computer and can call up any poem within seconds.

'Joining us today is Gary Dexter, he's a poet from Norwich, and he says he can recite any poem from memory...'

'Within reason,' I put in.

'Within reason, and he can take your requests. Gary, what got you into this?'

'I needed some money and I like poetry and I wondered if people would pay me for it. I had an eye condition so I couldn't use a computer so I started learning poems.'

'So what sort of poems do people ask for?'

'They tend to be poets who are long dead.' I'm standing up and pacing round and round my tiny bedroom. It has wooden floorboards and it occurs to me the noise of my footfalls might be quite loud. I stop. 'Kipling, Wordsworth, Shelley, Keats, and so on. Poets who rhyme.'

'What's the most popular poem?'

'Kipling. "If—".'

'Could you give us a burst of that?'

I do so.

'That was brilliant!'

'Yeah, I love Kipling. I suppose it's a complex poem, it has its dark side...'

'What do you mean?'

'Well it takes us to a time when life was simple, now there's a crisis in masculinity, nationhood, things are more complex.'

Dead silence. Actually this was a stupid, stupid thing to say because I have nothing further to add. Does he expect me to continue?

'Fair enough. OK, we've got some listener challenges here. Fred from Somersby wants to know if you can do "The Road Not Taken" by Robert Frost.'

'Sure.' I launch straight into it. I want them to know I'm not looking it up.

Two roads diverged in a yellow wood,
    And sorry I could not travel both...

I get to the end but then I somehow lose my way.

Somewhere ages and ages hence:
    Two roads diverged in a wood, and I –

I come to a grinding halt. The host steps in:

I took the one less travelled by,
    And that has made all the difference.

'Yes!' I say. 'Thank you! Failed at the final hurdle, sorry about that.'

'No, no! I've got a print-out here, so I'm reading it. That was amazing.' He seems genuine. It strikes me, as it has before, that, on radio at least, it is the getting it wrong

151

that is impressive, as long as most of it is right.

There's a trailer, then we're back. 'OK, we've got Gary Dexter here, a poet from Norwich, he performs in the streets and asks people what poem they want and then gives them a blast of it, we've got one from Emily in Horncastle. "The Charge of the Light Brigade" by Lord Tennyson.'

'OK, I can do that.'

'Go ahead.'

Half a league, half a league,
    Half a league onward,
All in the valley of Death
    Rode the six hundred.

Amazing how Tennyson starts when the charge has already begun. He could have started the action in a tent with a lot of maps, generals puffing on cheroots. But no – *in medias res*:

Plunged in the battery-smoke
    Right through the line they broke;
Cossack and Russian
    Reeled from the sabre stroke
Shattered and sundered.

The incomparable excitement of that blood-letting; the sabres flailing and hacking, chunks of muscle flying through the air, sticky wet lumps of flesh; the horses taking direct cannon hits and fountaining blood; gunner and mounted toff mangled and mingled; the screams of dying men under hoof or blade; stallions getting their nuts cut off; how very,

very enjoyable it all is; and it really happened, in 1854.

I put my all into it, shouting and grimacing into the phone.

'OK we're joined by Krimya. What did you think of that?'

'Yeah good!'

'What's the state of poetry at the moment as far as what you do is concerned?' asks the host. I presume this question is not for me, so I stay silent.

'Well poetry is the expression of people who want to find a better way. A better way of living.'

'Yes!' I interject, still on a bit of a high.

'Are your lyrics poetry?' the host asks Krimya.

'Call it what you like, it doesn't matter what you call it, it comes from the real experiences of people. That's why it's valuable. It's about what's going on now.'

'Would you agree with that, Gary?'

'Yeah of course I'd agree, my problem is with the poets who are on the traditional academic side of poetry, who produce verse that no one really cares about. They seem to think they have a monopoly on the truth about life, I just don't buy it and it doesn't have rhyme or rhythm, sorry to be saying this on Poetry Day, I love poetry but I just happen to think the best poetry was written a hundred years ago.'

'What do you think of that Krimya?'

'No no no no,' says Krimya. 'I like Shakespeare, don't get me wrong, I did Shakespeare at school...'

'What did you do?' I ask.

'*Twelfth Night.*'

'Oh yeah?'

'I can still remember bits of it. Let me speak a little,' says Krimya:

This youth that you see here
    I snatched one half out of the jaws of death;
Relieved him with such sanctity of love;
    And to his image, which methought did promise
Most venerable worth, did I devotion.

'Hoo!' Studio in an uproar.

    The host: 'Gary, can you match that?'

    'Er... hmm.'

    'OK.'

    'Well,' I say. 'Maybe at the end of *Twelfth Night*, or maybe it's in *King Lear*, there's a song:

He that hath and a little tiny wit
    With a hey, ho, the wind and the rain,
Must make content with his fortunes fit
    For the rain it raineth every day.'

Not such a big audience reaction.

    'Nice one,' says Krimya generously.

    'Are you going to give us some of your own stuff?' the host asks Krimya.

    Krimya does. Someone joins in beatboxing. It's good. Again, applause and cheers.

    The interview ends. I hang up and collapse onto the bed, where I lie mentally going over the exchange, wishing I hadn't sung-spoke Shakespeare in a quavering voice.

—∞—

THE POET: Emily Dickinson (1830-1886) was born and lived her life, mainly as a recluse, in Amherst, Massachusetts. She wrote prolifically, often in quatrains in which the words are separated by dashes – very few of her poems were published during her lifetime.

THE POEM: 'Because I Could Not Stop for Death' was published posthumously in 1890 under the title 'The Chariot'. Allen Tate said in 1936: 'This poem is one of the greatest in the English language; it is flawless to the last detail... Every image is precise and, moreover, not merely beautiful, but inextricably fused with the central idea.'

17

Because I could not stop for Death –

BY EMILY DICKINSON

Because I could not stop for Death –
   He kindly stopped for me –
The Carriage held but just Ourselves –
   And Immortality.

We slowly drove – He knew no haste
   And I had put away
My labor and my leisure too,
   For His Civility –

We passed the School, where Children strove
   At Recess – in the Ring –
We passed the Fields of Gazing Grain –
   We passed the Setting Sun –

Or rather – He passed Us –
   The Dews drew quivering and Chill –
For only Gossamer, my Gown –
   My Tippet – only Tulle –

We paused before a House that seemed
  A Swelling of the Ground –
The Roof was scarcely visible –
  The Cornice – in the Ground –

Since then – 'tis Centuries – and yet
  Feels shorter than the Day
I first surmised the Horses' Heads
  Were toward Eternity –

For me, poetry is able, with a single word, to change our perceptions, telling us things we already know but are hiding from ourselves; and the single word I would choose from this poem is 'strove'.

We passed the School, where Children strove
  At Recess – in the Ring –

Imagine the difference if Dickinson had written:

We passed the School, where Children played
  At Recess – in the Ring –

Striving is work, labour; and conventionally we see labour as the opposite of play. But in the playground, children compete against their playmates; separated from their loving mothers, and through painful trial and error, they learn of the realities of life. They journey toward adulthood.

They strive. And all the while Death has his eye on them.

This is a spectacularly grim poem, not just in its vision of humanity suffering and striving, but because of the sinister figure of Death, a bony Unter-driver, waiting to take us all, half-naked and shivering, to our final destination.

> The Carriage held but just Ourselves –
>   And Immortality.

Does Dickinson believe in this immortality? More unmortality than immortality, in a weedy grave surrounded by dead children. Is this the perspective from paradise?

> Since then – 'tis Centuries – and yet
>   Feels shorter than the Day
> I first surmised the Horses' Heads
>   Were toward Eternity –

A Polish guy in the street outside Pizza Express, Hackney – very young, very small, radiating energy. Furiously he questioned me. 'What is your outlook on life?' 'Do you have any interest in psychology or philosophy?'

'If you put that cigarette out,' I said, 'I will tell you.'

He threw the cigarette, which he had just that moment lit, into the street, tearing it from his mouth and flinging it from him, not looking where it was going. The street was crowded and it could have hit anyone. I looked at it lying there in the gutter, full-length, burning, and when

I looked back at my listener, he was regarding me with burning eyes.

'Well,' I said, 'I am – a materialist. Trapped by my own emotions.'

'What do you mean by that?' he inquired briskly.

'"All movement has a meaning/That is how it must always be seeming",' I recited.

'Explain what you mean.'

'Well, I believe only in material existence and yet my life is ruled by human emotions, love, desire, fear of death, so I never act on my materialism.'

'Why do you hold onto this materialism then?' he asked. 'Why not abandon it?'

My mind seized up. 'It seems the most rational,' I said lamely.

'It doesn't deal with any of the things that are important to you and yet you promote it as reality.'

I tried and failed to make any reply.

'You mention death,' he continued. 'What is death?'

'The end of life.'

'Yes, but what is the meaning of death. You say you live by meaning.'

'Did I say that?'

'"That is how it must always be seeming."'

Why had this Polish Socrates picked on me at the end of a hard day? Although actually he hadn't picked on me. I'd picked on him.

'Have you heard of Emily Dickinson?' I asked him.

'No.'

'She finds death in a flower, in children.'

'This interests me.'

'Would you like to hear a poem by her?'

'Go ahead.'

I recited 'Because I could not stop for Death.' For this very discriminating young man I tried to see the poem, and recite it, as if new for myself, as it was new for him.

'The Jews are quivering,' he said when I had finished. 'Is she Jewish?'

'No, no! "Dews"!' I say, horrified. "Dew"' – emphasizing the 'd' – 'is...'

'Yes, yes, water,' he said. 'I know this word. I thought it was uncountable. Like water.'

'Yes, it is uncountable,' I said. 'Normally.'

People are pushing in and out of the Pizza Express. It's drizzling. Presumably the young man's friends are in there somewhere, talking insatiably. I wondered what they could possibly be like. A cabal of émigré philosophers, remaking the world?

'It's a very good poem,' the young man was saying. 'She's alone with him in the carriage. This is a horse carriage I suppose, not a train carriage. An intimate encounter.'

'Exactly.'

'The grain gazes at them. It asks a question.' He gazed at me, burning.

'Yes,' I said.

'They come to a house which is a swelling in the ground. It is her new home. House/home. Polish does not have this distinction – there's no difference, it's the same word, *dom*.'

'Ah.'

'Yes, this is interesting. But what does it tell us about

death.' Metaphorically, he puts his index fingers together and leans back in his chair.

'She was a Christian,' I said. 'She believed in an afterlife. But the poem... the afterlife is an eternal looking back, for her, not a new beginning.'

'Yes.'

'So there is doubt in there, as well as faith. The greatest reality is extinction. It's close to us, all the time. As close as a lover.'

This was making a pretty good fist of it at 11:30pm and I was pleased with it. Some of the Polish guy's trenchancy had rubbed off. 'I think I should tell you,' I said (actually I'd told him already) 'that I'm a poetry performer. I do this for money.'

'I work here,' said the Polish guy, gesturing at the restaurant. 'In the kitchen. This is my cigarette break.' He glanced, for the first time, at the cigarette in the gutter. 'And now it's over. I'm sorry I haven't got any money for you. Stay if you like. I wish you good luck. Thanks for the poem.'

And with that he went into the restaurant.

THE POET: Charles Bukowski (1920-94) was a poet, short-story-writer and novelist (his novels include 'Post Office', 'Factotum' and 'Women') whose work closely mirrors his own life of heavy drinking, casual sexual encounters, and casual work.

THE POEM: 'Bluebird' is Bukowski's best-known poem, and explores, in brutal detail, the lengths we go to in order to hide our vulnerabilities. It appeared in *Last Night of the Earth Poems* (1992).

18

Bluebird

BY CHARLES BUKOWSKI

there's a bluebird in my heart that
   wants to get out
but I'm too tough for him,
   I say, stay in there, I'm not going
to let anybody see you.

there's a bluebird in my heart that
   wants to get out
but I pour whiskey on him and inhale
   cigarette smoke
and the whores and the bartenders
   and the grocery clerks
never know that
   he's
in there.

there's a bluebird in my heart that
   wants to get out
but I'm too tough for him,
   I say,
stay down, do you want to mess me up?
   you want to screw up the works?

you want to blow my book sales in Europe?

there's a bluebird in my heart that
    wants to get out
but I'm too clever, I only let him out
    at night sometimes
when everybody's asleep.
    I say, I know that you're there,
so don't be sad.
    then I put him back,
but he's singing a little in there,
    I haven't quite let him die
and we sleep together like that
    with our secret pact
and it's nice enough to make a man weep, but I don't
    weep, do
you?

Girl outside Tesco: That's a sad poem.
    Me: Yes it is.
    Girl: Are you an English teacher?
    Me: No.
    Although what, if I were an English teacher, would I be doing out here? Busman's holiday? Force-feeding poetry to the masses? I would have to be insane. Yet what I was doing didn't feel quite sane.
    Woman at party: What do you do?
    Me: At the moment I'm working as a poetry performer.

GARY DEXTER

Woman: Oh how exciting. Where do you perform?
Me: In the street. Public places.
Woman (puzzled): You mean, like busking?
Me: Yes, that's it.
Woman (not so excited any more): Oh.

Busking. You're going about your business and then this drop-out comes up to you and asks you if you have a favourite poem. Well, no, you don't have one. Or maybe you do, but it's none of his business. And why should you feel guilty for not giving him anything, for refusing to engage with him? You don't *feel like art* at the moment. You don't feel like cracking Netflix open. You don't feel like seeing a painting, contemplating a sculpture, hearing a symphony or listening to a poem, even if it's your favourite poem, because you're trying to get home and you are tired. You might not like how he recites it anyway. It might even ruin it for you. You *don't like buskers*. They interfere with your thoughts. They interfere with your anonymity. They interfere with your dreams.

And you interfere with theirs.

'Bluebird' was the most difficult poem I had to recite regularly, even though it is not the longest or the most difficult to remember. The problem is the tone. It cries out to be recited in an American accent, because the idiom is American ('whores', 'screw up the works', 'grocery clerks'), and yet if you recite it as an American, you bring falsity into the performance, no matter how good your American accent is. You cannot truly 'own' the performance by this method. So I tried reciting it in my own voice. Didn't work. I tried reciting it in a London accent (I'm originally from

167

North London). Better. I have some claim on that accent – it's the accent of my forefathers, although personally I'm more of an RP man. My North London tone was bitter and not a little vicious, but then thoughtful and half-despairing, as the poem obviously demands, ending on a direct question, my eyes flicking up into the eyes of the interlocutor. But it was never quite right, and I gave some truly awful recitations that even now I am ashamed of.

'Bluebird' is remarkable for being the only poem in the top 25 in free verse. 'Not Waving but Drowning' by Stevie Smith has free-verse aspects, but ultimately it's a poem in loose rhyming verses with a discernible rhythm. 'Bluebird' is unshackled by either classical rhyme or rhythm, and although it has structure in other ways it's breathtakingly free, a tour-de-force of freedom, deservedly in the top 25. It has a huge vogue among the young, some of whom have parts of it tattooed on themselves.

It's also a poem of powerful and opposing tidal forces. How could you pour whiskey on that poor bird? But don't we all? We must harden ourselves. We have to, or we would be just so much raw meat, quivering with agony at the stabbings we take. And yet we know the bird's in there, being tortured, and it breaks our hearts. As the girl outside Tesco's said, it's a sad poem. It's nice enough to make a man weep. But I don't weep. Do you?

Bukowski was really a 'grab 'em by the pussy' man, at least in his novels, where his protagonist is the Bukowski stand-in 'Chinaski'. Chinaski's method of chatting up sorority women is to go into the halls of residence well into the small hours and bang on every door in the corridor, screaming an enumeration of the size of his dick before collapsing in a puddle of vomit. His response to a sculptress who seems sorrowful is to tell her that he knows what's wrong with her, she's 'got a big cunt'. One of his favoured sex modes is to 'go into his rape act'. He never cleans his toilet because women don't want to see what a woman's house looks like, they already know what a woman's house looks like. The man is an anti-poetry poetry-man, a poet in full flight and revolt from poetry, a counter-Romantic and a poetry-hater. And yet this poem, 'Bluebird', was requested more by women than by men. Women admire Bukowski: they like his honesty and they like his vulnerability, and both are there in this poem, and neither of them are an act. Bukowski said that he drank so much before and during poetry readings because he was scared of the audience. Women appreciate Bukowski for the same reason they appreciate the writings of the Marquis de Sade. 'At least he's honest.'

Woman in beer tent: Do you know anything by Charles Bukowski?

Me: How about 'Bluebird'?

Woman: OK.

Me: [recites]

Woman: That was awesome! How did you do that? Hey, Jack, come and listen to this.

Jack: What?

Woman: This bloke can recite 'Bluebird.'

Jack: Yeah?

Woman: Do it again.

Me (to Jack, striking the business note): I'm a poetry

performer. I take requests and then if you enjoy it I offer my hat for any change you may have.

Jack: Go on then.

Me: [recites]

Jack: That was awesome! How did you do that? Hey, Katie, come and listen to this.

Katie: What?

Jack: This bloke can recite 'Bluebird'.

Katie: Yeah?

Jack: Do it again.

Me (to Katie, striking the business note): I'm a poetry performer. I take requests and then if you enjoy it I offer my hat for any change you may have.

Katie: OK. [etc.]

—◦◉◦—

It was, in some ways, more and more about the money. Love and disgust for poetry – disgust for the Augustans, rancour for the Romantics, malice for the moderns, venom for the Victorians – throbbed within me like Eliot's taxi, throbbing, waiting.

When I came through the door, late at night, my wife would emerge from her bed, where she'd been dozing with the light on, waiting for me to return. She would bring down the cardboard box that contained the money and the little bank-bags. I would flop into a chair, soaking up the room's warmth, and perhaps have a glass of beer, my first of the evening, joining, finally, the drunks with whom I'd spent the last few hours (pouring whiskey on my bluebird). And then Mimi would count up. When the pound coins were all arranged in Pisan towers of ten, it would be the turn of the 50ps, then the 20ps, then the 10ps, then the 5ps, then the 2ps, then the 1ps, then the foreign coins, which were put in a plastic strawberry punnet. To come home with £40 was good; £60 was better. One evening I came home with £109, my biggest haul ever. The money was my compensation for my own sense of shame and insult.

THE POET: William Henry Davies (1871-1940) was a Welsh writer who spent much of his life as a tramp, and who at the height of his popularity was lionized by London's literary establishment.

THE POEM: 'Leisure' was published in Songs of Joy and Others (1911), and represents nature-poetry at its most truly immersive; in comparison to Davies, Wordsworth seems like a mere weekend enthusiast. Many of Davies' poems, including this one, have been set to music by Sir Arthur Bliss.

19

Leisure

BY WH DAVIES

What is this life if, full of care,
  We have no time to stand and stare.

No time to stand beneath the boughs
  And stare as long as sheep or cows.

No time to see, when woods we pass,
  Where squirrels hide their nuts in grass.

No time to see, in broad daylight,
  Streams full of stars, like skies at night.

No time to turn at Beauty's glance,
  And watch her feet, how they can dance.

No time to wait till her mouth can
  Enrich that smile her eyes began.

A poor life this is if, full of care,
  We have no time to stand and stare.

There is something a little *off* about this poem. Its twee-ness grates. The personification of 'Beauty' as a seven-veils dancer is embarrassing. The squirrels hiding their nuts in grass are somehow risible. The inversion for the sake of a rhyme ('when woods we pass') is a tiny bit awful. It seems to cry out for parody. This was the worst poem – in my opin-ion – on my list. I didn't like it and I didn't like the people who liked it. I didn't like how they asked for it by calling it 'Stand and Stare.' 'Do you know "Stand and Stare"?' I particularly didn't like one skinhead market trader who asked me for it, and then, in the full knowledge that I was a poetry performer, refused to give me anything for it, even though he readily admitted he'd enjoyed it. Trade wasn't good.

I had given up on WH Davies. But then I chanced to read something about him. I was amazed to discover that he was perhaps the oddest poet on my list, an outsider-poet par excellence.

He was born William Henry Davies in 1871 in New-port, Wales. As a schoolboy, after becoming involved with a gang of roughs and acquiring a conviction for shoplifting, he began to write poetry. As he put it in his autobiography:

Having no knowledge of metre and very little of harmony, I composed and caused to be printed a poem describing a storm at night, which a young friend recited at a mutual improvement class, mak-ing after mention of the author's name, when I was publicly congratulated.

One of these early poems was 'Death':

> Beauty'll be no fairer than
>> Agèd dame so shrunk and wan,
> Whom she looks on proudly. Now
>> Did Death strike them sudden low.
> Strike them down, a little while,
>> Vanished Beauty's velvet smile,
> Ugly grinner she, and few
>> Mark the difference 'tween these two.
> Nothing here shall arbitrate,
>> Chivalry intimidate,
> Hour of doom, or change Death's laws;
>> Kings hire no ambassadors.
> Death makes monarchs grinning clowns,
>> Fits their skulls for bells, not crowns.

Capitalized Beauty in *this* poem is an 'ugly grinner'.

As a young man Davies left Wales for the United States, where he did odd jobs, begged, and worked on cattle boats plying their trade back and forth across the Atlantic. In America he took advantage of the system of 'boodle jails' whereby tramps could find overwintering accommodation in prisons by bribing corrupt officials. In 1899, in the company of a friend called Three-fingered Jack, he attempted to jump a freight train bound for the Klondike, and his foot was crushed:

> Even then I did not know what had happened, for
> I attempted to stand, but found that something had

happened to prevent me from doing this. Sitting
down in an upright position, I then began to exam-
ine myself, and now found that the right foot was
severed from the ankle.

The leg was amputated below the knee and for the rest
of his life he wore a wooden stump (like WE Henley,
that other two-initial one-poem one-leg man). Returning
to England, he began writing poems, trying to sell copies
door-to-door, which met with limited success. In 1905 he
put together a slim volume at his own expense, *The Soul's
Destroyer*. This he posted to famous people culled from
Who's Who, asking them to send the price of the volume by
return; many must have been put off by the lengthy Word-
sworthian 'growth of a poets mind' lyric that it opens with.
However, by this means he came to the attention of Arthur
Adcock, a journalist, who, though recognising that Davies'
poetry contained 'crudities and even doggerel' found in it
also 'some of the freshest and most magical poetry to be
found in modern books'. The volume went into several edi-
tions. Davies began to make friends in London's literary
world; his great gift was, it seems, not poetry, but he, him-
self. Prominent figures of the day were instantly taken by
him. George Bernard Shaw agreed to write the preface to
Davies' life-story *The Autobiography of a Supertramp* (which
gave its name to the '70s group Supertramp); Edward
Thomas helped him with accommodation; the Sitwells
developed a close friendship with him. Osbert described
him in his book *Noble Essences*:

At first sight, he appeared more Spanish than British in type. [He] seemed to belong to a race immeasurably old, perhaps to that ancient Pelasgian people from whom both Iberians and Celts claim to descend. His cast of face was rather long and aquiline, but with broad high cheek bones, and all of it, chin, mouth, long upper lip, nose, and high forehead, was finely sculptured and full of character. Features and hair both exhibited a naturally proud, backward slant or tilt, though there was no arrogance in him. His eyes were dark and gleaming, like those of a blackbird, and his skin possessed an almost nautical tinge. He was broad-shouldered and vigorous looking, but of less than middle height. Having lost a leg, he wore – for he could not afford the expense of a new metal limb – a heavy wooden stump, which made a wooden sound as he walked, and gave him a slow and very personal gait, making him raise and dip his shoulders as he moved.

He gave poetry readings with Hilaire Belloc and WB Yeats, and drew the admiration of as unlikely an experimentalist as Ezra Pound. He published indefatigably, writing verse, journalism, and the foreword to an edition of *Moll Flanders* (another tramp). His artist-friends included Augustus John, Walter Sickert and Jacob Epstein, who modelled a bust of him in 1917.

And after all this, 'Leisure' is the only poem of his that survives in the public consciousness. Again, rather similar to Henley, who would be utterly forgotten without 'Invictus'.

Impertinent of me, a mere performer, and someone with a mortgage and a bed to sleep in, to even begin to compare myself to a man who had no possessions and slept in barns, but I know what it is to *bother* people with poetry. One year was a bellyful. To spend one's whole life doing it: that requires something else, something so eccentric and self-believing that it merits a small entry in the DSM. People – and I apologise for pointing it out again – don't like beggars. They don't like pan-handlers who just need the bus fare to Cambridge, having lost all their money in some mishap; nor people sleeping on cardboard who may or may not be Syrian refugees. They block them out – *we* block them out – as soon as we catch a whiff of them, their booze-breath at 10 o'clock in the morning, their smelly clothes, their mutt-companions. But Davies lived this beggar's life, and these tramps, alcoholics, abandoned women, prisoners, the mentally ill, the drug-addicted and the diseased, were his friends. Along the way he found the time and space to become one of the most rapturous of all disciples of Nature, never losing his sense of the wonder of it, and expressing it in poetry full of pagan joy. One of my favourites is 'April's Charms':

When April scatters charms of primrose gold
    Among the copper leaves in thickets old,
And singing skylarks from the meadows rise,
    To twinkle like black stars in sunny skies;

When I can hear the small woodpecker ring
    Time on a tree for all the birds that sing;

And hear the pleasant cuckoo, loud and long –
   The simple bird that thinks two notes a song;

When I can hear the woodland brook, that could
   Not drown a babe, with all his threatening mood;
Upon these banks the violets make their home,
   And let a few small strawberry blossoms come:

When I go forth on such a pleasant day,
   One breath outdoors takes all my cares away;
It goes like heavy smoke, when flames take hold
   Of wood that's green and fill a grate with gold.

How can a man see so much misery – much more misery than we are used to seeing now, with people actually starving in the street, women mourning multiple child-deaths – and retain such a childlike delight? To go forth possessing nothing but the gold of the sun, to tramp and wake wet with dew, to spend hours just staring like a sheep or a cow?

I became a WH Davies convert.

THE POET: Lewis Carroll was the pen-name of Charles Lutwidge Dodgson (1832-98), mathematician, photographer, Anglican deacon and author of the Alice books. A prodigiously complex and clever man, Dodgson also invented the nyctograph, a tablet that allowed users to write in the dark.

THE POEM: 'Jabberwocky' appeared in *Through the Looking-Glass, and What Alice Found There* (1871), the sequel to *Alice's Adventures in Wonderland*. In the book, Alice finds the poem written in an unreadable script; holding it up to a looking-glass, she realises it is backwards. Mirrors and the paradoxes of optics are a recurring theme in Dodgson's work.

20

Jabberwocky

BY LEWIS CARROLL

'Twas brillig, and the slithy toves
   Did gyre and gimble in the wabe:
All mimsy were the borogoves,
   And the mome raths outgrabe.

'Beware the Jabberwock, my son!
   The jaws that bite, the claws that catch!
Beware the Jubjub bird, and shun
   The frumious Bandersnatch!'

He took his vorpal sword in hand:
   Long time the manxome foe he sought —
So rested he by the Tumtum tree,
   And stood a while in thought.

And, as in uffish thought he stood,
   The Jabberwock, with eyes of flame,
Came whiffling through the tulgey wood,
   And burbled as it came!

One two! One two! And through and through
   The vorpal blade went snicker-snack!

JABBERWOCKY

He left it dead, and with its head
   He went galumphing back.

'And hast thou slain the Jabberwock?
   Come to my arms, my beamish boy!
Oh frabjous day! Callooh! Callay!'
   He chortled in his joy.

'Twas brillig, and the slithy toves
   Did gyre and gimble in the wabe:
All mimsy were the borogoves,
   And the mome raths outgrabe.

If you put this poem into a spellcheck it comes up infested with wriggling red lines. However, there are two places where there should be red wriggling lines, but aren't: 'chortled' and 'galumphing'. That's because both these words were accepted into the English language shortly after the poem was published. 'Jabberwocky' may be the only poem in the English language that contains two successful neologisms.

I presume – though I don't know – that not many English nonsense poems are well known in other languages, due to translation difficulties. Not so 'Jabberwocky'. It exists in French (trans. Frank L. Warrin):

Il brilgue: les tôves lubricilleux
   Se gyrent en vrillant dans le guave.
Enmîmés sont les gougebosqueux

182

Et le mômerade horsgrave.

Latin (trans. Hassard H. Dodgson, Lewis Carroll's uncle):

> Hora aderat briligi. Nunc et Slythia Tova
>> Plurima gyrabant gymbolitare vabo;
> Et Borogovorum mimzebant undique formae,
>> Momiferique omnes exgrabure Rathi.

Japanese (trans. Mimi Dexter):

> Buririggu deshita. Suraibi tōbu
>> Wēbu de gairu to gimburu shite,
> Nante mimuji na borogōbu,
>> Mōmu rassu autoguraibimashita ne.

... and around 90 other languages, in hundreds of versions, partly because it features in the book *Through the Looking-Glass, and What Alice Found There*, which has itself been translated into many languages, but mainly because people love translating it. It may, in fact, be the most-translated poem in this book, with the possible exception of Shakespeare's 'Sonnet 18'. The fact that it's composed of words with no accepted meaning in English (apart from the explanation that Humpty-Dumpty gives them in the passage that follows in the book) should make translation a near-impossible task. But this fact actually gives license for a great deal of creativity; after all it's hard to be wrong when the meaning is not clear in English in the first place. A Japanese 'Jabberwocky' is particularly easy. Japanese contains so many English loan words – which are remodelled according to established rules – that the natural thing to do is simply to render all the neologisms into English-sounding borrowings.

Why has 'Jabberwocky' survived and thrived so? It's in the book, yes, but why has it found an existence outside the book? It's appeared in films, plays, comics, TV shows, video games and songs; there is (or used to be) a model of the Jabberwock in the London Dungeon, based on John Tenniel's illustration. I believe it's because its coinings, unlike in other nonsense poems, have linguistic depth.

The first version was written in 1855 as a parody of Anglo-Saxon verse, appearing in *Mischmasch*, a hand-produced publication that Carroll (or Dodgson, let's call him) wrote to amuse his family:

> Twas bryllyg, and ye slythy toves
>> Did gyre and gymble in ye wabe:
> All mimsy were ye borogoves;
>> And ye mome raths outgrabe.

When a girls' school in Boston asked Dodgson for his permission to name their magazine 'The Jabberwock', he satirically replied:

> The Anglo-Saxon word "wocer" or "wocor" signifies "offspring" or "fruit". Taking "jabber" in its ordinary acceptation of excited and voluble discussion, this would give the meaning of "the result of much excited and voluble discussion". Whether

this phrase will have any application to the pro-
jected periodical, it will be for the future historian
of American literature to determine.

So some of the linguistic echoes are Anglo-Saxon (or cod-
Anglo-Saxon). But there are others to listen for. Dodgson
was very specific on many details of the nonsense-words,
and this forms much of the interest of the poem. Asked
about 'uffish', he said that 'It seemed to suggest a state
of mind when the voice is gruffish, the manner rough-
ish, and the temper huffish.' The portmanteau word
'mimsy' came from 'flimsy and miserable'; the similar
word 'slithy' was derived from 'lithe and slimy'. (Dodgson
seems also to have invented the term 'portmanteau word',
without which we would have no term to describe 'spork',
'Oxbridge' or 'liger'.) 'Brillig' means 'four o'clock in the
afternoon, the time when you begin broiling things for
dinner.' A 'borogove' was, Dodgson said, 'an extinct kind
of Parrot. They had no wings, beaks turned up, made their
nests under sun-dials and lived on veal.' The pronuncia-
tion of 'borogove' was 'borrow-gove': Dodgson wrote in
the Preface to 'The Hunting of the Snark' that 'the first
"o" in "borogoves" is pronounced like the "o" in "bor-
row". I have heard people try to give it the sound of the
"o" in "worry". Such is Human Perversity.' A 'wabe' was a
'grass plot around a sundial', known as a wabe because it
'goes a long way before it, and a long way behind it.'
   Each coining gives off a sound like a struck bell.
Although Dodgson clearly made up many of the derivations
in retrospect, the words have a 'house style' of their own;

they feel compatible with one another. Not all nonsense is equal. As Alice says after reading the poem: 'Somehow it seems to fill my head with ideas – only I don't exactly know what they are!'

———

Reciting 'Jabberwocky' was usually very enjoyable. I'll never forget the astonishment on one man's face when he groped for an elusive memory of the poem, which he'd last heard in childhood – 'something about slimy toathes' – and then found I could recite it all.

Perhaps my most surreal Jabberwocky encounter was with a very drunk man and his friends on some steps in an alleyway at midnight. The drunk man was dressed in a pirate costume and was drunk in a way that is not often seen: he was ecstatically drunk, almost incapable of speech, his eyes seeming to shine as if their vitreous bodies had been replaced with neat vodka; he was in bliss. I asked the group what poem they wanted, and the drunk man replied (with difficulty): 'Jabberwocky'.

It turned into a duet. I recited the first line, he the second, and so on; and as we recited, shouting and gesticulating, he had such cruel difficulty articulating that only his passion for the poem was able to get the better of his incapacity:

'Twas brillig, and the slithy toves
　Da gharrra gibuh inna wayp!
All mimsy were the borogoves,
　Anna momerassss owgrayp!

'Beware the Jabberwock, my son!
　Jozza by, clozza cash!
Beware the Jubjub bird, and shun
　Froom-yush bannersnassshh!'

There ought to be a drunk version of 'Jabberwocky' to add
to all the other translations, if it doesn't exist already.

THE POET: Christina Rossetti (1830-1894) was born into an intensely creative London family: her brother was the painter/poet Dante Gabriel Rossetti, and another brother and sister, William and Maria, were also writers. She is best known for the long poem 'Goblin Market' and for 'Remember'.

THE POEM: 'Remember' is a sonnet on the theme of death and remembrance, written in 1849 when Christina was nineteen. By this time she was already an accomplished poet (her first poem, her brother William later recorded, was composed before she could even write, and contained the lines 'Cecilia never went to school/Without her gladiator').

21

Remember

BY CHRISTINA ROSSETTI

Remember me when I am gone away,
   Gone far away into the silent land;
When you can no more hold me by the hand,
   Nor I half turn to go yet turning stay.
Remember me when no more day by day
   You tell me of our future that you plann'd:
Only remember me; you understand
   It will be late to counsel then or pray.
Yet if you should forget me for a while
   And afterwards remember, do not grieve:
For if the darkness and corruption leave
   A vestige of the thoughts that once I had,
Better by far you should forget and smile
   Than that you should remember and be sad.

Formerly a paradise for buskers of all kinds, Covent Garden has succumbed to the blight of amplification. Everyone, whether musician, comedian, juggler or miscellaneous mountebank, has a public address system. An arms race has taken place. No one can *not* be amplified, without paying the financial price. The result: unamplified me is unable to make his wares audible without screaming, which reduces the effect somewhat of, say, 'Pied Beauty' by GM Hopkins.

After an hour of failing to collar anyone, I ran into two girls in matching uniforms loaded up with promotional bottles of fizzy water, who, after some bemusement, asked for Christina Rossetti. Specifically 'Goblin Market'.

'I'm afraid I don't know that one,' I shouted. 'But I know another one by Christina Rossetti.' And then my mind froze. 'You know the one.'

'No, which one?' one of them shouted back.

'You know the one,' I said. 'About death. Her death.'

They shook their heads.

'Oh, God,' I said. 'It's about how she's got this guy and when she dies she writes this sonnet for him.'

They regarded me with polite discomfiture, a pissed uncle who had failed to pull off a conjuring trick.

'"Goblin Market,"' repeated one of them, loudly. 'It's the only one I know.'

Actually all I needed was the first line, and I would be off like a rocket. I knew the poem very well: it was the first poem I had ever learnt. Fourteen lines only. I had recited it in the street, on the radio, to myself in the bath a million times, but now, in cacophonic Covent Garden, it utterly eluded me.

'Sorry,' said one, 'We've got to get on.'

They walked away with their bottles; and as soon as they were out of earshot, the first line came back to me with photographic clarity: 'Remember me when I am gone away.'

My howl of four-letter anguish was drowned out by a nearby guitarist playing 'Walking on Sunshine'.

--❧--

It strikes me that there is something very strange about this poem. I don't think people understand it. They ask for it as if it were a love poem: 'Remember me when I am gone away.' It has a certain morbid voluptuousness, as in a Pre-Raphaelite portrait: a beautiful woman in a black velvet dress, with shining golden hair, consumptive but still entrancing, her youth contrasting piquantly with the mouldering stones among which she wanders.

But look closely at the poem and it is (unless I am going mad) full of resentment. 'Remember me when I am gone away... when you can no more hold me by the hand.' Nothing wrong so far. Except... whereas it's often nice to be held by the hand, what if the speaker actually wants to get away, and begrudges being held by the hand, as a child is held? Why does she turn to go, but then, turning, stay? What coercive control keeps her from leaving? Then:

Remember me when no more day by day
    You tell me of our future that you plann'd:
Only remember me; you understand
    It will be late to counsel then or pray.

This seems to me to be getting grimmer. 'You tell me of our future that *you* plann'd.' Never mind what I wanted; you planned it. And when I'm gone, 'It will be late to counsel then or pray.' You will no longer be able to counsel me, which could be considered a euphemism for 'give me unwanted advice' or even 'control me'; nor will you be able to force me into any pointless devotions. 'It will be too late to pray.'

The above may seem a stretch, but in the sestet the author makes herself plainer:

> Yet if you should forget me for a while
>   And afterwards remember, do not grieve:
> For if the darkness and corruption leave
>   A vestige of the thoughts that once I had,
> Better by far you should forget and smile
>   Than that you should remember and be sad.

In other words: when I die, going into 'darkness and corruption' (no radiant afterlife here, note; so much for the purposeless 'praying' of the preceding lines), it will be a good thing if you forget me, because if you were to remember (or find out, somehow) what I really thought, you would be sad. Why? Because I resented you for the control you exercised over me. (There is no mention of love anywhere in the poem, so this would seem to follow.) The only thing you did was to make plans for me as I tried to leave. So don't remember, for your own sake. After all: if even a 'vestige' of the thoughts that I once had would make you sad, then surely the full truth, in all its uncensored frankness, would ruin your life.

Well, it's one way of looking at it.

The biographical detail behind the poem is intriguing. Rossetti was only nineteen years old when she wrote it in 1849, living at home with her three talented siblings, one of whom was the poet/painter Dante Gabriel Rossetti. She was the object of romantic interest from more than one eligible young man, but resisted marriage. Instead she devoted herself to poetry, and in fact, in later life, became the best-known Victorian woman poet after Elizabeth Barrett Browning. According to her brother William, she had extreme facility in composition: the siblings played a game, *bouts-rimés*, in which they raced to compose a sonnet with a given rhyme-scheme. Christina could turn out sonnets literally within a couple of minutes. (Imagine her on a Victorian version of Britain's Got Talent.)

Looked at in this light, 'Remember' is not necessarily the outpouring of Christina's own feelings. As an accomplished and self-assured poet, she may have been channelling any one of a number of different characters: her own father perhaps, who was seriously ill at the time. It may even have been a particularly successful *bouts-rimés* exercise. Christina was by no means near death – she was nineteen years old and had more than four more decades yet to live. The 'Me' and 'I' of the poem are, likely, personae. The plain fact of the matter is that in poetry – in books, in general – not everything narrated in the first person is *necessarily* about the author.

Personally I prefer a simpler poem, entitled 'Song', written in 1862. No one ever asked me for it, but it does, I think, contain the sort of sentiment people *think* they are getting when they ask for 'Remember':

REMEMBER

When I am dead, my dearest,
  Sing no sad songs for me;
Plant thou no roses at my head,
  Nor shady cypress tree:
Be the green grass above me
  With showers and dewdrops wet:
And if thou wilt, remember,
  And if thou wilt, forget.

I shall not see the shadows,
  I shall not feel the rain;
I shall not hear the nightingale
  Sing on as if in pain:
And dreaming through the twilight
  That doth not rise nor set,
Haply I may remember,
  And haply may forget.

THE POET: Thomas Stearns Eliot (1888-1965) was born in St Louis, Missouri, and lived for most of his life in England. Publisher, playwright, essayist and poet, he was a tangential member of the Bloomsbury Group, and married twice, on both occasions to women whose names began with 'V'.

THE POEM: 'The Love Song of J Alfred Prufrock' (1915) delineates the hesitations and self-doubt – and, even above these, the sexual paralysis – of a shadowy member of a cultured and probably monied social set in the early years of the twentieth century.

22

The Love Song of
J. Alfred Prufrock

BY TS ELIOT

Let us go then, you and I,
   When the evening is spread out against the sky
Like a patient etherized upon a table;
   Let us go, through certain half-deserted streets,
The muttering retreats
   Of restless nights in one-night cheap hotels
And sawdust restaurants with oyster-shells:
   Streets that follow like a tedious argument
Of insidious intent
   To lead you to an overwhelming question …
Oh, do not ask, "What is it?"
   Let us go and make our visit.

In the room the women come and go
   Talking of Michelangelo.

The yellow fog that rubs its back upon the win-
dow-panes,
   The yellow smoke that rubs its muzzle on the win-
   dow-panes,

THE LOVE SONG OF J. ALFRED PRUFROCK

Licked its tongue into the corners of the evening,
  Lingered upon the pools that stand in drains,
Let fall upon its back the soot that falls from
chimneys,
  Slipped by the terrace, made a sudden leap,
And seeing that it was a soft October night,
  Curled once about the house, and fell asleep.

And indeed there will be time
  For the yellow smoke that slides along the street,
Rubbing its back upon the window-panes;
  There will be time, there will be time
To prepare a face to meet the faces that you meet;
  There will be time to murder and create,
And time for all the works and days of hands
  That lift and drop a question on your plate;
Time for you and time for me,
  And time yet for a hundred indecisions,
And for a hundred visions and revisions,
  Before the taking of a toast and tea.

In the room the women come and go
  Talking of Michelangelo...

I remember my feelings on first encountering this poem.
I was sixteen, and it was baffling. I sensed in the poem an
intelligence utterly beyond my own, and, more than that, a
fully-formed literary personality. I didn't know a great deal

about poetry at the time; I think I had started writing my own poems, flounderingly.

Perhaps Prufrock could have shown me the way towards my own style, inspired me; but no, not a bit of it. The poem awed me, cowed me, and finally depressed me. The poem was an alp, a trackless desert, and not a desert on this planet, but on a moon of Jupiter. Prufrock was beyond me, in every way. It was almost like encountering a completely new art form, as if the poem were not really a poem at all (rather like the first time I heard Philip Glass, which I thought was a signal to test the radio). Even the character of Prufrock was inaccessible to me, despite the fact that he was, like me, a failure, uncomfortable in his own skin; but he was a failure and uncomfortable in his own skin in a way that I knew that I could never be.

What made this worse was that hard on the heels of reading Prufrock, I chanced upon a parody of the poem, by a schoolboy. This boy couldn't have been much older than I; conceivably, he was younger. His parody had been published in an anthology of schoolchildren's poems and was by far the best thing in it. This schoolboy, my contemporary, had comprehended the poem, possessed the poem sufficiently to actually mock it! My sense of humiliation knew no bottom. The parody read wonderfully well. Instead of coffee spoons the boy had used balloons or spittoons or some such thing; instead of having Prufrock declaim in rhyming couplets 'No! I am not Prince Hamlet, nor was meant to be', he had made him say 'No! I don't want any ham yet, for my tea.' I don't remember the details. It was all extraordinarily clever and I knew that such a thing was, for me, completely impossible, in the same category as asking a girl out or publicly speaking before an audience that included my headmaster.

Now, at a ripe old age, I can look back at that 16-year-old self and smile. Or perhaps not. In some ways the poem is as mysterious as ever. Having studied it at university, I can see all the things that anyone can see who has merely mined it for its allusions, and I have, I hope, an understanding of its pivotal role in literary modernism. Having learned it by heart (it's a long poem, long enough to make you hoarse), I can also see how its rhyme and metre and structure work, and am aware, in a way I wasn't before, that if there is one thing Prufrock isn't, it's free verse. But at the core of it still is a wonderful strangeness. In its form and tone it is without precedent in English; in its handling of metaphor it is new and exciting; in its daring shifts of register, and in its willingness to mislead, it is exhilarating and perplexing. I suppose such poems come along once every generation, or every two generations. And such mystery can never truly die.

Imagine reading it for the first time in 1915. That's what Ezra Pound did, and he was amazed. (By God, Ezra knew a thing or two!) He wrote to Harriet Monroe, editor of the US magazine *Poetry*, saying that the poem was the dawn of an entirely new mode of literature. Eliot, he said, in Blastian capitals, 'has actually trained himself AND modernized himself ON HIS OWN. The rest of the promising young have done one or the other, but never both.' Monroe concurred, and gave Prufrock a world premiere in the issue of June 1915. Without Prufrock there might have been no collaboration between Pound and Eliot, and thus no 'Waste Land', at least not in the form we have it.

Because of Prufrock, 'The Waste Land', and related poems, Eliot's literary influence in the 1920s was immense, as we know. Some felt it to be rather pernicious. There is a story of one magazine editor who automatically binned every poem that contained reference to broken columns, dry sand, or any mention of the words dream, dull, water, rock, dry, dark, fire, hollow, dead, light or stone. Ernest Hemingway, in mourning over the death of Conrad in 1924, wrote petulantly that if he could bring Conrad back to life 'by grinding Mr. Eliot into a fine dry powder and sprinkling that powder over Conrad's grave in Canterbury', he would 'leave for London early tomorrow morning with a sausage-grinder'. (It was always *Mr* Eliot; even Orwell called him *Mr* Eliot.) Christopher Isherwood wrote of Eliot's overpowering influence on the young Auden:

> While Auden was up at Oxford he read T. S. Eliot... the earliest symptoms of Eliot-influence were most alarming. Like a patient who has received an over-powerful inoculation, Auden developed a severe attack of allusions, jargonitis and private jokes. He began to write lines like: 'Inexorable Rembrandt rays that stab...' or 'Love mutual has reached its first eutectic...' Nearly all the poems of that early Eliot period are now scrapped.

—⁕—

In a sense, Prufrock was the centre of my career as a poetry performer: it was the longest poem I learned in complete form, and the one I was most proud of remembering. Every invitation to recite it was a marathon; I had to be in tip-top shape, sober as a Jesuit, and ready to explore, to find, if possible, something new, each time – to MAKE IT NEW, as Pound would say.

I can remember every time I performed it. One of the strangest was to a young man in front of a very loud portable sound system (the sound system was strapped to a furniture trolley) in a park. The young man had scars on his face that may have been the remnants of very bad acne or possibly the result of some sort of collision in which he was dragged along a road for some distance; he was also stoned out of his mind and pissed to boot, reeking of marijuana fumes and holding a can of Oranjeboom. He asked for the poem, and I said, as I always did, 'What, all of it? You realise it takes ten minutes?' But yes, he wanted all of it, and so I began, though I had literally to shout. The customer is always right. Around the tenth line or so I realised that the young man was actually mouthing the words along with me, and in fact, seemed to be slightly ahead of me at points, so that if I paused for effect, he would dive in. The music was so loud it was difficult to hear him. So we recited the poem together, on and off. He had been smoking dope and drinking beer but still he had perfect recall. For me this would have been out of the question.

On another occasion, Alan, a teacherly type, young, bespectacled, heavy-set, and very sure of the ground he was standing on, asked me to take it from 'I should have been a pair of ragged claws' to the end, which is about 500 words. Perhaps he was aware that Prufrock was a long poem and he didn't want me going on all night – or perhaps he just didn't think I could remember it all. We were standing outside a pub in Broadgate, and an attractive young woman was standing with him, possibly a girlfriend, though something suggested that she was just be a work colleague. Alan had confidence but not allure.

As I recited, Alan insisted on correcting me twice, and he was right on both occasions. The first was in the rather tricky 'Hamlet' monologue, which starts off so assertively – 'No! I am not Prince Hamlet, nor was meant to be', and then descends, through various Poloniusesque modulations, into uncertainty:

> At times, indeed, almost ridiculous—
> Almost, at times, the Fool.

It isn't difficult to get the 'almosts', 'indeeds' and 'at timeses' mixed up with one another.

'You're making it up!' Alan snorted when I put a foot wrong. 'It's not "Indeed, at times, almost ridiculous", it's "At times, indeed, almost ridiculous".'

I stopped. 'I don't make poems up,' I said.

'All right, go on,' said Alan.

I did so, but then got to the lines:

> Shall I part my hair behind? Do I dare eat a peach?

'"Do I dare *to* eat a peach,"' said Alan.

I stopped again. 'No, it's "Do I dare eat a peach".'

'I'm sure it's "*to* eat a peach".'

Something began to make me think that this was for the benefit of the young lady, who was standing with a bottle of Becks and not saying anything.

'No, sorry,' I said, 'It's "Do I dare eat a peach". 'It's like "Do I dare disturb the universe". There's no "to".'

This knocked him back a bit, and while he was formulating a reply I said: 'Look it up when you get home.' I went on to finish the rest of the poem. Alan, to give him credit, was appreciative. We had a brief chat.

When I got home I looked it up, and I was right. It said 'Do I dare eat a peach.' No 'to', in my edition anyway. But then I felt a small doubt. That's what it said in *my* edition, but my edition was not really an edition, as such. It was *The Nation's Favourite Poems*, edited by Griff Rhys Jones, published by BBC Books. I ought to check. Where, though, to check? Each edition might have a different version. Which would be definitive? The answer was clear: the first edition, in *Poetry* magazine of June 1915, the world premiere that Pound had organized for Eliot. I needed – impossible wish – a facsimile copy.

Immediately, however, I was granted that wish. *Poetry* is still going, and it has an impressive website with archive material and facsimiles of early editions. I found the June 1915 edition and scrolled through to the last page of the poem.

'Do I dare to eat a peach?' it said.

—❦—

THE POET: Stevie Smith (1902-71) was originally Florence Margaret Smith, and got the name 'Stevie' when a friend remarked that she looked like the jockey Steve Donoghue. In addition to poetry she wrote three novels. Her work was admired both by the public and the literary world, particularly by writers such as Philip Larkin and George Orwell.

THE POEM: 'Not Waving but Drowning' appeared in the collection of the same name of 1957. It deals, as does much of her poetry, with death, filtered through a bleakly humorous apprehension of English middle-class gentility: the poem is, after all, couched in terms of what 'they said'.

23

Not Waving but Drowning

BY STEVIE SMITH

Nobody heard him, the dead man,
    But still he lay moaning:
I was much further out than you thought
    And not waving but drowning.

Poor chap, he always loved larking
    And now he's dead
It must have been too cold for him his heart gave way,
    They said.
Oh, no no no, it was too cold always
    (Still the dead one lay moaning)
I was much too far out all my life
    And not waving but drowning.

This is one of those poems that I understood better after I had learned to recite it. You see, it incorporates three voices. The first might be called the 'narrator'. She it is who says:

Nobody heard him, the dead man,
    But still he lay moaning

Then there is the 'dead man' himself, speaking from beyond death:

> I was much further out than you thought
>   And not waving but drowning.

The third voice is plural; it is what 'they' say:

> It must have been too cold for him his heart gave way
>   They said.

The voice of 'they' must be different from the voice of the 'narrator', because it is the 'narrator' who reports what 'they' said. Yet none of the poem is given in speech marks, so it all flows together. To recite the poem, it is necessary to give recognition to each of these three voices, by changing gear at the transition between them, bringing out how uncomprehending and faintly uncaring 'they' are, how futile and sad the dead man is, and how spectral and mysterious the narrator is ('Nobody heard him, the dead man').

'Not Waving but Drowning', in which a 'dead man' is able to talk, a poem about death-in-life, or life-in-death, in which even the other characters in the poem seem to float, disembodied (for how else can 'they' speak in unison, if not in some ghostly chorus?) is an unsettling read. It is by no means unique in Stevie Smith's work. Smith (the narrator in the poem?) was preoccupied with death and suicide from an early age – from seven years old, by her own account. Many of her poems address these realities, death being, as she said, 'the only god who comes when he is called.' She said about 'Not Waving but Drowning':

> I read about a man getting drowned once – his friends thought he was waving to them from the sea but really he was drowning. This often happens in swimming baths or at the seaside – and then I thought that, in a way, it is true of life too: that a lot of people pretend, out of bravery really, that they are very jolly and ordinary sort of chaps but really they do not feel at all at home in the world or able to make friends easily, so they joke a lot and laugh and people think they're quite alright and jolly nice too but sometimes the brave pretence breaks down and then, like the poor man in this poem, they are lost.

On one occasion I came across a group of five or six lads, teenagers really, outside a pub called The Birdcage. One of them, a freckled lad, asked for 'Not Waving but Drowning', and I recited it without a hitch. But after it was over, none of them seemed to want to pay up. No one wanted to make the first move. Neither did they seem to want to leave or go back into the pub.

Then we had a strange conversation which, though not unique, struck at the heart of why I was there in the first place.

'What's the point of it?' said a bearded fellow in a white T-shirt with a legend saying 'Greatly'. He wasn't the one who'd asked for the poem.

'What's the point of what? The poem?' I asked.

'I understand the poem,' he said. 'But what's the point of it?'

'Poems stimulate your emotions,' I said. 'They call forth an emotional response.'

'What's the point of that?'

'It gives you pleasure. Or it makes you look at life differently.'

He frowned. Another one tried a different tack. '"Not Waving but Drowning",' he said. 'Is that supposed to be about something?'

What a question. It seemed that the freckled lad who had asked for the poem was somewhat untypical of the gathering. He was a soft-looking type, small, and his companions didn't think much of his taste.

'What do *you* think it's about?' I asked, stalling for time.

'What do *you* think it's about?' he replied.

'There's more than one way of drowning,' I said. 'People drown throughout their lives but there's no one there to see.'

Not impressed. 'Are you drowning?' asked someone.

'Yeah, I drown every night.' No one was smiling.

Another question: 'You said you offer your hat for any change. I don't have a change of hat.'

Comedians.

'I need a new one,' I said.

'You need some new poems.'

'What poems do you want to hear?' I asked.

'I'm not interested in poems. Had enough fucking poems at school.'

'OK, see you then.'

'Hey. Give us your best poem.'

'I've got a poem about your mum,' said one to another, meditatively.

'No, it's all right, I don't think you'd enjoy it,' I said. My best poem was 'The Daffodils' by Wordsworth.

'Spit some grime.'

Oh God.

'"Not Waving but Drowning",' said one.

I thought of the *Private Eye* cover from the 1980s that showed Michael Foot in a donkey jacket, waving his stick, and subtitled 'Not Waving but Drowning'. Michael Foot was dead now. It was a very long time ago.

The only solution was actually to go into the pub. That way I could be sure of getting away from them. I did so.

Standing at the bar I ordered an orange juice, then walked into a part of the pub used for music performances. An audience were sitting on plastic chairs or on the floor waiting for a band to come on in the brownish dark. On the way in I stumbled over a drink that had been put on the floor, knocking it over.

'Oh, shit,' I said to the girl sitting near it. 'I'm really sorry. Let me get you a new one.'

'That's OK,' she said.

'No, really,' I said. (It was stupid to put a drink on the floor in a dark room, but still.)

'OK, it's a quadruple rum and coke. And one for him,' she said.

I went to bar to order the drinks (singles not quadruples) and there I met a female I vaguely recognised.

'Oh, the poetry guy!' she said.

'Yes,' I said.

'How's business?'

'Could be better. I just did "Not Waving but Drown-ing",' I said.

'Oh, I love that poem. Stevie Smith. That's my name.'

'Stevie Smith?'

'No, Stevie.'

'Want to hear the poem?' I asked.

'I know it already.'

'OK, you recite it to me then. If you can do it I'll give you a quid.'

She did so, word perfect.

I handed over the quid, paid for the drinks, and then took them to the people in the brownish bar. The music had still not started. I asked who was coming on. I felt an adamantine certainty that if I stayed, the band would suck any remaining sense of my own identity out of me.

When I got back to the bar, Stevie wasn't there.

Leaving, the lads were also nowhere to be seen.

I was ten quid out of pocket, and it was a freezing night in December. All the restaurants had shut, and as I walked down Bridewell Alley there was no one about. Everyone had gone home, except the club-goers in Prince Of Wales Road, and they were not the most appreciative audience for poetry.

I didn't feel I understood the poem I had recited, nor did it 'call forth an emotional response' in me except tiredness.

So I went home.

—⊶⊙⊷—

THE POET: John Donne (1572-1631) was one of the Metaphysical Poets, along with Andrew Marvell, George Herbert, Henry Vaughan and others. He was also an Anglican divine, and as well as his early erotic poetry wrote much religious verse.

THE POEM: 'The Flea' was published after Donne's death in 1633. Donne argues that the flea, by biting both the woman and her potential seducer, has already rendered sexual intercourse a *fait accompli*, since the 'mixing of bloods' (which was believed to occur during sex) has already happened within the flea's body.

24

The Flea

BY JOHN DONNE

Mark but this flea, and mark in this,
  How little that which thou deniest me is;
It sucked me first, and now sucks thee,
  And in this flea our two bloods mingled be;
Thou know'st that this cannot be said
  A sin, nor shame, nor loss of maidenhead,
  Yet this enjoys before it woo,
    And pampered swells with one blood made of two,
  And this, alas, is more than we would do.

Oh stay, three lives in one flea spare,
  Where we almost, nay more than married are.
This flea is you and I, and this
  Our marriage bed, and marriage temple is;
Though parents grudge, and you, w'are met,
  And cloistered in these living walls of jet.
  Though use make you apt to kill me,
    Let not to that, self-murder added be,
  And sacrilege, three sins in killing three.

Cruel and sudden, hast thou since
  Purpled thy nail, in blood of innocence?

Wherein could this flea guilty be,
    Except in that drop which it sucked from thee?
Yet thou triumph'st, and say'st that thou
    Find'st not thy self, nor me the weaker now;
    'Tis true; then learn how false, fears be:
      Just so much honour, when thou yield'st to me,
    Will waste, as this flea's death took life from thee.

Donne's flea is an outlier: the earliest mass-appreciated poem after Shakespeare. I suppose people value Donne because of his fusion of the amatory and the cerebral. There is charm in the discovery that, in distant epochs, people were just as obsessed by sex, and as prone to innuendo, as we are now. 'Call country ants to harvest offices' as Donne puts it in 'The Sunne Rising'. Or in 'The Good Morrow':

    I wonder, by my troth, what thou and I
      Did, till we loved? Were we not weaned till then,
    But sucked on country pleasures, childishly?

Again the Hamlettian pun on 'country'. There's an awful lot of sucking in Donne. (Even more than in Sir John Suckling.) In 'The Flea', of course:

    It sucked me first, and now sucks thee.

Donne's love-poetry exemplifies the fact that the best

love-poetry is usually about something in addition to love and bawdry. 'The Flea' is about a sexy flea-hunt through mounds of infested clothing, yes, but also, with a certain blasphemous daring, the Trinity:

Oh stay, three lives in one flea spare

... and the redemption of Mankind through Jesus Christ:

Cruel and sudden, hast thou since
    Purpled thy nail, in blood of innocence?

It seems that love-poetry, to achieve turbo-levels of intensity, should combine love with other considerations. And not just for humorous effect. In 'The Love Song of J Alfred Prufrock' Eliot gives us love and anxiety (or sexual paralysis); in 'In My Craft and Sullen Art' Dylan Thomas pits love against art. But the greatest pairing, repeated over and over in love poetry, is that of love and death, the meaning-generativity of love vs the meaning-destructivity of death, locked forever in combat. In Keats' 'Bright Star', in Vera Brittain's 'Perhaps', in Marvell's 'To His Coy Mistress', or in Leo Marks's 'The Life That I Have', to name but four, death gives shape to love by opposing it.

─◦◉◦─

When I think of 'The Flea', I think of a couple who were obviously in the early stages of love. They were also old, in their late fifties or early sixties: it would not have been

THE FLEA

the first time they had loved, and perhaps it had crossed
their minds that this might be the last. They were about to
enter a posh English dining establishment in Cambridge
at about eight o'clock in the evening, and may have been
on a first date: hope shone from them. Both were thin and
refined-looking, the woman small, thin and refined-look-
ing, and the gentleman tall, thin and refined-looking. They
could have been members of a string quartet, probably
both violins, though either might have been a violist. Nei-
ther looked strong enough to manage a cello.

I asked them whether they'd like to hear a poem.

'Do you know anything by John Donne?' the man
replied, possibly expecting to catch me out.

'How about "The Flea?"' I said.

'Oh, yes please,' said the lady.

I began. They listened avidly. These were cultured
people.

Mark but this flea, and mark in this,
    How little that which thou deniest me is.

That opening: Donne setting out his stall. Donne exhib-
iting the flea, trapped between thumb and forefinger, to
demonstrate the pettiness of what is being denied him.
Donne the irresistible seduction-machine. Had either one
of these two people before me recently done any denying
of the other, or were they both already un-done? They cer-
tainly had the glow of the recently done.

Though parents grudge, and you, w'are met

218

And cloistered in these living walls of jet.

Parents? All four of their parents were probably dead, or very old. No matter. For the purposes of love and of Donne, we are eternal teenagers.

Just so much honour, when thou yield'st to me,
   Will waste, as this flea's death took life from thee.

I.e. none at all. Donne's matchless handling of the cae-sura, and the repeated hammer-blows of 'honour', 'waste', 'death' and 'life' as he brings the poem off, were almost too much for them in their already-heightened state, and at the poem's conclusion the lady let out a tiny groan. She fumbled at her handbag. All of a sudden she looked ill; had the poem genuinely had been too much? Had it moved her in some way that I had not calculated, and indeed never try to calculate? The lady had no money for me, nor a handkerchief for herself, nothing of any help, and she snapped the clasp shut. She looked old. The gen-tleman took her arm. Gaiety had evaporated; here was some trauma rising from the past that none of us had pre-pared for. What could it have been? An old lover? A dead friend? That word, 'death'? Or was it merely that my deliv-ery had been disappointing?

'Excuse us just a moment.' The man led her without a word into the restaurant. I watched while they stood talking to a waitress in the lit window and pondered on the futility of what I was doing, in general. The conversation, obviously about tables, drinks, etc., was taking a while, and I turned to go, giving up on them. Walking ten steps I encountered another group of people, this time three fat and healthy youngsters. I became cheery again. 'Excuse me, can I ask you something?'

All of a sudden the tall, thin, refined-looking man was breathlessly at my elbow. 'I just wanted to give you this,' he said, handing me a ten-pound note.

—◦◦◦—

THE POET: Sir John Betjeman (1906-84) was Poet Laureate from 1972 to his death in 1984. His German-sounding name was actually of Dutch origin. He was a great champion of Victorian architecture, and his statue stands in St Pancras station, which he helped to preserve.

THE POEM: Betjeman met the real-life Joan Hunter Dunn in 1940 and fell in love. The poem – the details of which are imaginary – was published in *Horizon* magazine in 1941, and Betjeman invited Joan for lunch, presenting her with a copy of the magazine. Joan Hunter Dunn did marry, becoming Joan Jackson, and lived in Singapore and Rhodesia.

25

A Subaltern's Love Song

BY JOHN BETJEMAN

Miss J. Hunter Dunn, Miss J. Hunter Dunn,
    Furnish'd and burnish'd by Aldershot sun,
What strenuous singles we played after tea,
    We in the tournament – you against me!

Love-thirty, love-forty, oh! weakness of joy,
    The speed of a swallow, the grace of a boy,
With carefullest carelessness, gaily you won,
    I am weak from your loveliness, Joan Hunter Dunn.

Miss Joan Hunter Dunn, Miss Joan Hunter Dunn,
    How mad I am, sad I am, glad that you won,
The warm-handled racket is back in its press,
    But my shock-headed victor, she loves me no less.

Her father's euonymus shines as we walk,
    And swing past the summer-house, buried in talk,
And cool the verandah that welcomes us in
    To the six-o'clock news and a lime-juice and gin.

The scent of the conifers, sound of the bath.
    The view from my bedroom of moss-dappled path

A SUBALTERN'S LOVE SONG

As I struggle with double-end evening tie,
    For we dance at the Golf Club, my victor and I.

On the floor of her bedroom lie blazer and shorts
    And the cream-coloured walls are be-trophied with
    sports,
And westering, questioning settles the sun,
    On your low-leaded window, Miss Joan Hunter
    Dunn.

The Hillman is waiting, the light's in the hall,
    The pictures of Egypt are bright on the wall,
My sweet, I am standing beside the oak stair
    And there on the landing the light's on your hair.

By roads 'not adopted', by woodlanded ways,
    She drove to the club in the late summer haze,
Into nine-o'clock Camberley, heavy with bells
    And mushroomy, pine-woody, evergreen smells.

Miss Joan Hunter Dunn, Miss Joan Hunter Dunn,
    I can hear from the car park the dance has begun,
Oh! Surrey twilight! importunate band!
    Oh strongly adorable tennis-girl's hand!

Around us are Rovers and Austins afar,
    Above us the intimate roof of the car,
And here on my right is the girl of my choice,
    With the tilt of her nose and the chime of her
    voice,

And the scent of her wrap, and the words never said,
And the ominous, ominous dancing ahead.
We sat in the car park till twenty to one
And now I'm engaged to Miss Joan Hunter Dunn.

Philip Larkin called Betjeman 'Betjers', and loved and admired the man and his poetry. Betjeman was Larkin's senior by sixteen years, so Betjeman was a sort of elder-brother figure to Larkin. A comparison of their two lives is interesting. Betjeman composed in traditional forms, particularly blank verse, when such forms were long out of style; so did Larkin. Both disliked modernity in archi-tecture or art. Both went to Oxford. Both were much concerned with loss, death and the past. Both mourned the vacuum left by Christianity, Betjeman as a believer and Larkin as a non-believer. Betjeman filled his poetry with conscious archaism, capitalizations and Augustan con-tractions even when they were unnecessary to scansion or sense ('Fill'd', 'track'd'). Larkin pushed all this aside but did not condemn it, in Betjeman at least. There was off-hand racism in the make-up of both men: 'He pinions me in that especial grip/His brother learned in Kobë from a Jap,' Betjeman says in his poem 'Original Sin on the Sussex Coast'. Never mind that 'Kobe' does not have an umlaut, or even a macron, on the final 'e': here is the imperialist experiment in all its casual disdain.

If there is a common thread in the poetry of both, it is that of *longing*; for the past, for a lost England, for a countryside before it was covered by concrete and tyres, for sex that didn't happen. (Betjeman on being asked towards the end of his life what, if anything, he regretted, said: 'I wish I'd had more sex'.) Betjeman is in love with hard-bodied Olympic athlete girls: they are tousled, toned, magnificent, hieratic; he is crumpled, old, bald, smelly, mouldering. Larkin is in love with the 'bosomy English rose' but is stuck with 'her friend in specs I could talk to'.

Larkin, I would guess from the way he is now taught in schools, is in the ascendant. He has survived the furore over his trunkful of schoolgirl flagellation porn and has been reappraised by his latest biographer as a carefree lover of life. Betjeman, however, is beginning to look seriously out of date. He has to survive something much more serious than a spanking: his poetry is full of the impedimenta of a vanished world: the English hymnal, ladies playing on the hautbois, Sturmey-Archer gears. His poetry speaks of a particular English social class, the upper-middle, that was shrinking and losing influence even while he was writing. These days we cannot really be expected to sympathize when he speaks of 'the pictures of Egypt' that are 'bright on the wall'. How were those pictures of Egypt obtained? By taking the bread from the mouths of Egyptian children, insulting Egyptian women, and dispossessing Egyptian men. The whole edifice of Betjeman's world, roads not adopted, woodlanded ways, mushroomy smells and all, is only possible through the exploitation of a) the workers and b) our colonial slaves. Did Betjeman know this and was ironizing it? The picture is mixed. There is certainly much gentle mockery of the lives of the upper-middle, as in his poem 'In Westminster Abbey':

Think of what our Nation stands for,
    Books from Boots and country lanes,
Free speech, free passes, class distinction,
    Democracy and proper drains.
Lord, put beneath Thy special care
    One-eighty-nine Cadogan Square.

With these lines and others in mind we can justifiably seek class ironies in 'A Subaltern's Love Song', but if they are there, they are very well hidden: the ironies we find are less ironies of class than ironies about the silliness of young love. The final line – 'And now I'm engaged to Miss Joan Hunter Dunn' – has a note of faint terror in it, it seems to me. There is nothing in the poem that leads us to doubt that Betjeman loved this particular social class, approved of it and the people who inhabited it, and was sorry to see its erosion.

On the streets, no one younger than 60 ever asked me for a poem by Betjeman. And even a 60-year-old would be hard pushed to remember Lyon's Corner Houses and the Euston Arch. More often these respondents would be in their 70s or 80s, and would have memories of Betjeman's TV programmes in the late 1950s and 60s about Norfolk churches or Metroland. They were often slightly moth-eaten, and turned out to have a good working knowledge of English poetry, two things that of course go together. They also knew that Miss Joan Hunter Dunn was a real person of that name, who died in 2008 aged 92, so it was pointless telling them.

I remember reciting this poem to a very odd family,

almost a parody of the upper-middle classes, encountered coming out of the Globe Theatre on the South Bank. The mother had beaverish front teeth and was wearing a print dress that hung limply from her. Her daughter had a decided odour of ponies; her son, like boys of any class, was deathly pale and looked as if he had been prised from the internet by force. They listened graciously, gave me a pound or two – and then the mother asked me:

'Who's your favourite poet?'

'Larkin,' I said.

'Oh, he's so gloomy though, isn't he?'

'I don't know...' I said. I struggled to remember a happy poem by Larkin. I couldn't. 'Actually yes, you're right, he is gloomy.'

'Not like Betjeman.'

So this lady was actually setting up a contrast between Larkin and Betjeman.

'They were friends,' I said. 'I think they shared a certain outlook on life.'

'Well,' said the woman. 'They may have been. But Betjeman is so funny...'

'Yes...'

'He's a satirical poet really.'

'Really? I don't see him like that, I see him as a poet of loss. After all, that poem we've just had is about a girl who he never met...'

'Ah, but he did meet her,' she said gently. 'He sent her the poem and they met for lunch.'

'Oh. I didn't know that.'

'Yes, and he was married at the time, which was naughty

of him. She studied at Queen Elizabeth College where my mother studied. Only it wasn't called Queen Elizabeth College then, it was called King's College of Household and Social Science.'

'Oh. Really?'

'Yes. People got up to all sorts of things during the war, you know.'

Suddenly 'Betjers' was having lots of illicit sex with tennis Rhine-maidens *and* writing funny poems about it. He hadn't had as much sex as he'd wanted, true – but then Casanova probably said the same thing. Betjeman was young and good-looking in those days. Not like Larkin at all, who never rose above toad-level, was permanently sexually frustrated, kept a 'wank-book' and grew up in a council house. I had misinterpreted the link between them. There wasn't one. Betjeman was her poet and the poet of her children and class, she knew more about him than I did. Larkin was an *arriviste*.

'Well, thank you. Come along!' she said to her children. 'We have to catch a train.'

—◦◉◦—

THE POET: Leopold ('Leo') Marks (1920-2001) was a writer and cryptographer who ran the codes office for the Special Operations Executive (SOE) during the Second World War. After the war, Marks worked as a playwright and screenwriter.

THE POEM: Marks wrote the poem in 1943 about his girlfriend Ruth, who had died in a plane crash. The poem was one of the original compositions memorized by agents of the SOE in order to decrypt communications. 'The Life That I Have' featured in the 1958 film *Carve Her Name With Pride*, about the SOE agent Violet Szabo.

26

The Life That I Have

BY LEO MARKS

The life that I have
  Is all that I have
And the life that I have
  Is yours.

The love that I have
  Of the life that I have
Is yours and yours and yours.

A sleep I shall have
  A rest I shall have
Yet death will be but a pause.

For the peace of my years
  In the long green grass
Will be yours and yours and yours.

—◦⊙◦—

I would usually leave home at about 8pm, when people
were on their way to restaurants or to the pub. By 10pm
my clientele were considerably merrier; by 11:30 they

were staggering and singing; by 1am the middle-aged had surrendered the streets to the young. I often felt like a schoolteacher in a playground of rowdy children, except that some of these children were bigger than me. No push-chairs; no elderly; only girls and lads out to get hammered with their mates. And policemen.

I remember one man I met in Lower Goat Lane at about 12:30am. He had a hungry look and he was on his own. He seemed, unusually, completely sober. He asked me for a poem that would help him seduce a woman. 'Seduction poem, eh?' I said, feeling witch-doctorish. 'Try Leo Marks. "The Life that I Have". It starts like this:

> The life that I have
>   Is all that I have
> And the life that I have
>   Is yours.'

He frowned, taking it in. I went on to the next verse:

> The love that I have...

'No, that'll do,' he said. 'OK, let me just get this. "The love that I have, of the life that I have..."'
'No, the life that I have, is all that I have...'
'Yeah, you put me off. The life that I have, of the...'
'The life that I have, is all that I have...'
'The life that I have, is all that I have...'
'And the life that I have...'
'And the life that I have...'

'Is yours.'
'Is yours.'
'Very good,' I said. 'Now put it together:

The life that I have
    Is all that I have
And the life that I have
    Is yours.'

'OK,' he said. 'OK...

The life that I have
    Is all that I have
And the life that I have
    Is yours.'

'Yeah!' I said. 'You got it.'

'Brilliant,' he said, giving me three quid. He took fewer than ten steps before bawling into the ear of the first woman who came past:

The life that I have!
    Is all that I have!
And the life that I have!
    Is yours!!!

I made a hasty departure. I don't give refunds.

The popularity of this poem mystified me a little. I knew it had something to do with codebreaking and the Second World War, so I looked it up, and it turned out to be to do with the Special Operations Executive in occupied France. It was actually a fascinating story. The poem was one of a number that had been written as keys to aid SOE agents in encryption and decryption. It had featured in a 1958 film, *Carve Her Name with Pride*, about Violette Szabo, an SOE spy. Was this, then, why the poem was so popular?

No, it wasn't. I discovered the real reason when I got married. Prospective married couples in UK registry offices are given a book of permissible readings, short texts that may be read out during the ceremony. One of these was 'The Life that I Have'. It was being read at weddings up and down the land.

I often had cause to explain the story about the war and the poem-codes. One of these occasions was outside a beer festival late one summer night. I was talking to a young man who was very drunk. He had probably been drinking all day. Within the first minute of our conversation he told me that he was a PhD student. He was obviously proud of it, and had no inhibitions left. I asked him what he was studying.

'Physico-chemical biology,' he said.

'Wow,' I said. 'Physico-chemical biology. Is that a real subject?'

'Yes,' he said. 'But no one understands it.'

'Well, let me tell you what I do,' I said, getting down to business. 'I recite poems. You choose one, and I try to remember it. If I get it right you have to pay me.'

'I don't know any poems,' he said pleasantly. 'But go on, tell me one.'

'All right,' I said. 'How about this one. It has a very interesting story. It might appeal to you. It's all about maths.'

'Go on.' He was swaying a little, and his friends had deserted him, but he was in a condition where time no longer really mattered and he felt comfortable hearing a poem.

I recited 'The Life that I Have'.

It ended. I waited for a reaction.

'I don't get it,' he said.

'Well,' I said, 'it's a love-poem, isn't it? The poet says his life, and his love, are all for her. And even when he is dead, his life will have been only for her. It's simple. It's beautiful. But,' I raised a finger, 'there's a little more too it. It's about maths, as I said.'

'K.'

'The poem dates from the Second World War. When we were fighting the Nazis. We sent a number of spies over there to gather information, in occupied France. Many of these spies were young women. Young Englishwomen. We needed to communicate with them while they were in France, and they needed to communicate with us. But the Germans had broken all our codes. We needed some new codes that the Germans couldn't crack. So one man, Leo Marks, invented the poem-code. And this is one of the poems he used. He wrote it himself.'

The young man swayed. He seemed to be listening.

'Now,' I said. 'The way that it worked was that if the message was something like "HITLER WILL BE IN PARIS", for example, we would first need to encode the letter "h".

For "Hitler". So we'd look at the poem and we'd find the first "h". It's actually the second letter of the poem. It's the second letter of the word "the". So we'd send the digits 1, 2, meaning line 1, letter 2. OK. Now the next letter we need is "i". We look in the poem for the first incidence of that, and give the appropriate numbers. And so on.'

I knew that this was a very grave over-simplification of the encryption method, but there was no point in burdening him with too much detail. The basic idea was there.

'The beauty of it,' I continued, 'is that the poem was never written down anywhere. The agent memorized it, just like I've memorized it. And it wasn't in any book, because Leo Marks made it up. So the Germans could never find the key. See?'

'No,' said the young man with conviction. 'No. I don't get it.'

I could feel the swarf being shaved from my patience. The pound coin that was probably all he would give me seemed a distant prospect. In fact, I would soon have to remind him what this recitation-for-money business was all about, because he had almost certainly forgotten.

Keeping my annoyance in check, I repeated the whole explanation again, in full.

'See?' I said.

'No,' said the young man, just as definitely.

'Jesus Christ, it's simple!' I said. 'I thought you were a PhD student!'

'I am,' he said. 'I'm studying physico-chemical biology. No one understands what it is, so I don't blame you.'

'Well *I* blame *you*,' I said. 'You don't seem to understand what I'm talking about, and I'm explaining it in words of one syllable. It couldn't be simpler.'

The young man seemed hurt. He was a very nice young man. Then his friend turned up.

'Hey, where have you been?' the friend said.

'Talking to this guy,' the young man said.

'I'm reciting a poem to him,' I said, taking charge.

'About what?'

'It's about the Second World War,' I said. 'All right, I'll explain it to you,' I said to the friend. 'Let's see if you get it. Then maybe you can tell me if I'm going crazy or not. All right, we were fighting the Nazis, right? The Nazis. We sent agents over to France...'

I went through the whole thing.

'Do you understand?' I asked.

'Yeah...' he said, a little defensively.

'OK, maybe you can explain it to him then,' I said.

'All right,' said the friend. He turned to the young man. 'OK, the agents memorized the poems and they used the poems to code the messages so they knew what they wanted them to do.'

'Yes,' I said. 'That is it. In a nutshell.'

'Eh?' said the physico-chemical biologist. 'How can you use a poem to code a message? I'm confused. I don't get it. I'm not stupid, you know.'

He was looking at me quite plaintively, but his brain had been destroyed by alcohol. He was a physico-chemical biologist but now he wasn't really one at all; he was just an idiot, a person incapable of understanding the simplest thing, and it frightened him a little.

'All right,' I said, taking a deep breath. I could feel a return of the hysteria that would sometimes begin to build when I had to explain to my son, aged five, for the tenth time, why he couldn't have a go with the electric lawn-mower. 'I am going to tell you one more time. I want you to listen very carefully. This is the last time. OK? Now, it's to do with the war. The Second World War. We had to communicate with each other using codes so our plans would be secret. But the Germans could intercept our messages. So we had to find a way to make sure they couldn't break the codes. Do you understand?'

The young man goggled at me, swaying. His friend was also swaying. They were like twin yolks in an amniotic sac.

'Yes,' the young man said after a time.

'Now... one man found a way to do it. He wrote a poem, and he told the agent, the spy, to memorize the poem. Got it so far?'

'Got it.'

'Then if he wanted to send the spy a secret message, he took the first letter he needed, and he found one that matched it in the poem. He gave that letter-position a number. OK?'

'Mmm.'

'And he sent them that number. So they knew which letter he meant, didn't they? Then he went through the message doing the same thing, until the message was finished. "KILL HITLER", or whatever. Do you see?'

The young man's face expressed the sort of puzzlement one sometimes sees in the face of a cat that has heard a dog on the radio.

'No,' he said.

'Oh, FUCK!' I screamed. 'OK, goodnight.' I began walking away.

'No, no,' cried the young man, coming after me. 'Come on, I just don't understand! Explain it to me! Come on!'

But I kept going.

I hope now, for the sake of physico-chemical biology and the miracles it performs for us, that this young man has stopped drinking.

THE POET: John Masefield (1878-1967) was Poet Laureate from 1930 until his death in 1967, one of the longest tenures of the office. He wrote children's novels and poetry, and served as a hospital orderly in World War One.

THE POEM: 'Cargoes' was published in 1903, and describes, in three verses – with no introduction or editorializing – three ships, each carrying a different cargo: one from Babylon, one from Spain, and one from Britain, each journey separated by hundreds of years. The poem is a masterclass in the use of rhythm and sound.

27

Cargoes

BY JOHN MASEFIELD

Quinquireme of Nineveh from distant Ophir,
   Rowing home to haven in sunny Palestine,
With a cargo of ivory,
   And apes and peacocks,
Sandalwood, cedarwood, and sweet white wine.

Stately Spanish galleon coming from the Isthmus,
   Dipping through the Tropics by the palm-green
   shores,
With a cargo of diamonds,
   Emeralds, amethysts,
Topazes, and cinnamon, and gold moidores.

Dirty British coaster with a salt-caked smoke stack,
   Butting through the Channel in the mad March
   days,
With a cargo of Tyne coal,
   Road-rails, pig-lead,
Firewood, iron-ware, and cheap tin trays.

CARGOES

Masefield was poet laureate from 1930 to 1967, but today is known for only two poems, 'Cargoes' and 'Sea Fever', which goes like this:

> I must go down to the seas again, to the lonely sea and the sky,
>> And all I ask is a tall ship and a star to steer her by...

... and which was about number 31 or 32 on the list of most-asked-for.

'Cargoes' is notable for an extremely unusual and complex metrical structure. Each stanza opens with a line of two feet of four syllables each, called paeons – *very* unusual – followed by two trochees (two-syllable feet with a stress on the first syllable, DA-dum). Here's the first line of the first stanza, with the stressed syllables in capitals:

> QUINquereme of NINeveh from DIStant OPHir

And here's the first line of the third stanza:

> DIRTy British COASTer with a SALT-caked SMOKE stack

The same pattern is evident in each.

The second lines of each stanza are similar to the first lines, with one difference: they have each had one syllable lopped off, and one syllable strengthened to make what is called a molossus, or three-stress foot. In the case of the second stanza, second line:

242

Dipping through the tropics by the PALM-GREEN
SHORES

Here 'PALM-GREEN SHORES' is a molossus. And
Masefield didn't stop there; he loved his molossi, being
something of a molossus man; a colossus of the molossus,
in fact. Each stanza ends with one:

SWEET WHITE WINE.
GOLD MOIDORES.
CHEAP TIN TRAYS.

He might as well have called the poem 'Molossi' because
the extraordinary rhythmical effect of those three foot-
stamps. Would the poem be known and loved without
them? I think not.

(I am reminded of a story by the Edwardian humorist
Saki, 'Cousin Teresa'. The main character dreams of writ-
ing a successful musical play. He doesn't have much idea
about the plot or the characters, but knows that it will fea-
ture a little girl leading a procession of dogs. The song that
accompanies the dog-parade will feature the words: 'Cousin
Teresa takes out Cæsar, Fido, Jock, and the big borzoi.'
Three bass-drum beats will accompany the syllables 'big
borzoi'. Friends express scepticism that this will be enough
to guarantee success, but when the play is staged, the whole
of London goes wild for it, and the playwright receives a
knighthood. And why? Because of that molossus!)

In terms of its subject-matter, 'Cargoes' presents three different ships, one per stanza. The first is a 'quinquireme', or galley with five banks of oars, bound for Nineveh in Babylonia; so we must assume we are in the Ancient Near East, circa 1000 BC. The second ship is a 'stately Spanish galleon'; we have jumped forward 2500 years to the age of European empires, diamonds, gold moidores (Portuguese coins), and puffy shirts. The third is a much-debased vessel; a 'dirty British coaster', self-soiled by its smoke, chugging by steam-power through the channel, presumably on its way out from Britain to the rest of the world, carrying the products of Britain's industrial efforts: Tyne coal, road-rails, pig-lead, iron-ware, cheap tin trays.

The attempt is to contrast the romance of ancient sea-journeys with the grime and utilitarianism of the present-day; poetry versus prose, in fact. And yet... from our vantage-point in the early twenty-first century, surely those cheap tin trays and road-rails seem as exotic as the apes and peacocks of Babylon or the diamonds and amethysts of Spain. The poem has acquired an irony Masefield may not have anticipated. It was published in 1903, at the height of Empire, before the First World War, when Britain really did make everything, export everything and have a size-eleven foot in everything. ('Cargoes' was written in the same decade as 'If –' by Kipling.) In a twenty-first-century Britain still struggling with its post-industrial identity, such mastery (*they* want *our* cheap tin trays, *we* make the rails for *their* trains) is difficult to imagine.

The poem urgently needs updating with a fourth verse featuring a new 21st-century vessel. What could it be? A ferry, complete with whining obese children? A floating cruise liner so vast that it contains five iMax cinemas? But these wouldn't quite fit the bill, because we need a 'cargo'. So we are probably looking at a container ship, laden with imports from the Far East:

> With a cargo of sports shoes,
>   Dildoes, iPhones,
> Flight-socks, fake furs, and cat-flea sprays.

Let's show Masefield some *real* debasement.

First you love them; then you anthologize them; rarely, if ever, do you forgive them. Masefield is unforgiven and fading fast. He suffers from 'poet laureate syndrome'. Many poet laureates, historically, were distinctly sub-par appointments, given the job for political reasons, and are often remembered with outright mocking laughter: Thomas Shadwell, the butt of Dryden's 'MacFlecknoe'; Colley Cibber, the Dunce of all Dunces; and the poetaster-general Henry James Pye. Masefield, though he got the job on merit (as far as I know), is often sniffed at for his general conventionality, his facility, his Edwardian melodiousness; he is a sort of greetings-card poet. The critic WH Hamilton said in 1922 that Masefield's work was characterized by 'pretty jingles of rime and curiosities of design like the well-known "Cargoes", which cannot boast one finite verb.' No finite verb? I suppose that is true, but it is an odd criticism.

The key verbs 'rowing', dipping' and 'butting' are superbly planned and placed. Masefield's real crime was to make no intellectual demands on the reader, which, in the post-war world of 1922, struggling with the new urgencies of modernism, was simply old-fashioned.

The only people who asked me for 'Cargoes' were in their later years, and could probably remember poetry as it was taught (and remembered) at school in the 1950s and 1960s, when the poem was still popular (that molossus!). On radio, callers would often request 'Cargoes', and then proceed to try and recite it. They had put in many grim hours learning it fifty years ago and weren't going to let this go to waste. But merely articulating its syllables is tough ('Isthmus', 'amethysts', 'quinquireme'), and Masefield makes extensive use of alliteration and assonance, so that some lines are veritable tongue-twisters. If anyone tried to recite it, I would happily give them enough rope:

Me: 'Go ahead.'

Caller (tremulously): 'Quinkareen of Nineveh from distant Opha... Hoe-ing Rome to haven in Sunny Palestine... er...'

Or

Caller: 'Dirty British coaster with a smoke-caked saltstack...wait a minute... a smoke-caked smoke-stack...I mean a salt-coked stope-sack...I mean a...'

Me (laconically): Can I help you with that?

Sometimes only a professional will really do.

—⊕—

THE POET: Philip Edward Thomas (1878-1917) was an essayist, novelist, poet, critic and journalist. He was a good friend of Robert Frost, who lived in England at the time; they often took long walks together. Frost write his poem 'The Road Not Taken' after observing Thomas's indecisiveness about which path to take.

THE POEM: 'Adlestrop' was written in 1915. Adlestrop is a real place in Gloucestershire. The railway station no longer exists, although the line itself (the Cotswold Line) is still in use.

28

Adlestrop

BY EDWARD THOMAS

Yes. I remember Adlestrop –
    The name, because one afternoon
Of heat the express-train drew up there
    Unwontedly. It was late June.

The steam hissed. Someone cleared his throat.
    No one left and no one came
On the bare platform. What I saw
    Was Adlestrop – only the name

And willows, willow-herb, and grass,
    And meadowsweet, and haycocks dry,
No whit less still and lonely fair
    Than the high cloudlets in the sky.

And for that minute a blackbird sang
    Close by, and round him, mistier,
Farther and farther, all the birds
    Of Oxfordshire and Gloucestershire.

This poem's genesis, according to Thomas's notebooks, occurred at 12:45 on the afternoon of the 24th of June 1914, when the down train made a stop at Adlestrop station. Adlestrop is a real place in Gloucestershire, and although the railway station no longer exists (it was closed by the Beeching cuts in 1966) there is still a village there, with a church and shop.

The 24th of June 1914 was, of course, just before the outbreak of the First World War, and it was in that war that Thomas was killed. Something about the stillness and heat of that summer day, a timeless moment in which the train itself is slumbering and the only sound is birdsong, draws people to this poem; they are drawn too because they know that Thomas was to die in the trenches. In fact, the war had already started by the time he began writing the poem in 1915, which was also the year he joined up. He died in 1917. For the reader, his death seems, horribly, to be lurking there in the tranquil lines.

My personal opinion is that it would be pointless to make a pilgrimage to Adlestrop, even though the village exists. I don't imagine you would find anything there that you couldn't find in a million other places. People, of course, go there anyway. They tell me it's a nice village, and that even now, although there's no railway station, there's a nice bus stop with a plaque featuring some words from 'Adlestrop'. But if they expect to feel what Thomas felt, surely they might as well stay at home and sit in their gardens. There's no point going to see the willows, willow-herb, and grass. These things can be seen anywhere. Adlestrop is everywhere, or nowhere.

It seems to me that the poem is at least partly about proper nouns. Adlestrop: an ungainly name, a concrete, a man-made name; and one that contrasts almost comically with the ungraspable quiddities of sky, space, earth and nature that we find in the main body of the poem. Thomas's train stops; there is silence, broken by an occasional throat-clearing from a fellow passenger (a concert-goer coughing between movements); and, as often when encountering real stillness and solitude (without a book, newspaper or mobile phone to fall back on), a certain sense of bafflement creeps up on the poet, along with a natural attempt to grasp meaning in this world of skies and trees and weeds, a world of which we are at least nominally a part; but that meaning inevitably eludes him, just as it generally does us. It is a poem in which nothing happens, either in the trainscape or the poet's mind. No revelation, no argument, no conclusion. And then, finally, in the last line, the reader, having witnessed this failure to extract meaning from life, is abandoned, none the wiser, in the company of two further solid and all-too-human proper nouns: 'Oxfordshire and Gloucestershire' (two regimental names, as it happens, furthering the idea that this is, in some sense, a war-poem). Proper nouns which sweetly stake a claim to portions of the earth's surface, and which, like Adlestrop, represent our human attempts to bind and tame mystery.

In the final analysis, though, we are humans, not black-birds. And since we are humans, names have power over us, and poetry is the business of using this power. You can only work with what you've got.

I was often aware of using words as powerful tools, and in particular, nouns: names, proper names, and places. Nouns have an ascendancy over other parts of speech, which is strange, because we think of verbs as 'doing' words, and of action as having the most power. But no, it is nouns that are truly indispensable.

I remember one afternoon when I learned of the power of nouns, and how they work to give power to poetry. Two encounters in London, separated only by minutes.

The first experience was with two men vaping outside a bar in the early autumn evening. One of them requested, and got, 'Jerusalem' by William Blake. It is, in some ways, very similar to 'Adlestrop': both are poems with four verses composed of four lines of iambic tetrameter (four feet that have the rhythm da-DUM), and both have a place-name as their title and mention place-names as talismans of belonging. Giving me money, my client congratulated me: 'You're doing a great thing there, we need more people like you, it's fantastic. Keep it up.'

No proper nouns, no payment, I thought as I walked away.

The second experience was perhaps ten minutes later. This time it was a middle-aged couple sitting on some steps by a fountain. The man was compact and handsome; his female companion dourer, older than him, her nose in a book. I asked them whether they wanted a poem, and the man seemed taken with the idea, mentioning 'Adlestrop'. I recited it.

However, the woman was not pleased. As I recited, she seemed to grow increasingly unhappy, and when I finished, it was as if I had stolen something from her. By invoking 'Adlestrop' I had hurt her, somehow, taken some of her own power, something of her own self-respect, and she wanted it back. She could only get it back by diminishing me.

'Hey!' she said. 'That was really good.'

'Thank you,' I said.

'The beggars are getting more cultured.'

'Ah hah.'

'Yes, thank you,' said the man.

'Let me see if I can find something for you,' she said. 'She looked in a purse and found twenty pence. 'There,' she said, examining my face, 'will that do?'

'I think I might have something,' said the man.

'It's OK,' said the woman, motioning him to desist. She had another quick rummage. 'Here,' she said, 'I've got another ten pence.'

She smiled, for the first time.

'Thank you,' I said.

'Right,' she said. They got up and dusted themselves down. She stowed her book in her bag. They walked away, the man looking back over his shoulder.

I sat down where they had been sitting, weighing the thirty pence in my hand, and reflecting, as I often did, that art could often feed parasitically from the life-force of its audience.

On a good day.

THE POET: John Keats (1795-1821) was a medical doctor and poet who died in Rome aged only twenty-five; by that time he had produced a large body of work and many hundreds of letters. Among his most famous poems are 'Ode to a Nightingale', 'To Autumn' and 'On First Looking into Chapman's Homer'.

THE POEM: 'Bright Star' (begun around 1817-19) is one of the best-loved love-sonnets of Keats, and may have been written primarily for Fanny Brawne. Keats' friend Joseph Severn said that the last draft of the poem was transcribed by Keats into his copy of Shakespeare's works, aboard the ship Maria Crowther in 1820, when sailing on his final journey to Rome. Its first publication was in the prosaic-sounding *Plymouth and Devonport Weekly Journal* in 1838, seventeen years after his death.

29

Bright Star

BY JOHN KEATS

Bright star, would I were stedfast as thou art –
　　Not in lone splendour hung aloft the night
And watching, with eternal lids apart,
　　Like nature's patient, sleepless Eremite,
The moving waters at their priestlike task
　　Of pure ablution round earth's human shores,
Or gazing on the new soft-fallen mask
　　Of snow upon the mountains and the moors –
No – yet still stedfast, still unchangeable,
　　Pillow'd upon my fair love's ripening breast,
To feel for ever its soft fall and swell,
　　Awake for ever in a sweet unrest,
Still, still to hear her tender-taken breath,
　　And so live ever – or else swoon to death.

An extraordinary poem, sometimes billed as 'the last poem
Keats ever wrote'. However, it was certainly not, since Keats
finished a version of it at least two years before his death in
1821. As in the sonnet 'When I have fears that I may cease
to be' (possibly the second-most-commonly asked-for Keats

poem), 'Bright Star' derives its power from its simultaneous treatment of both love and death. It gives an ultimatum to the forces that rule the universe – either let me lay my head on her breast forever, or let me die.

Keats was closely involved with two young women during his short life, either of whom (or both of whom) could have provided the pillow mentioned in the poem. The first was Isabella Jones, a beautiful and cultured young woman who Keats met in 1817. The second was the one more often associated with 'Bright Star', the 18-year-old Fanny Brawne, who Keats met a year later, became betrothed to, and with whom he had a voluminous correspondence. He certainly gave a copy of the poem to Fanny Brawne as a love-token.

The position of 'Bright Star' at a relatively lowly number 29 does not take into account the true popularity of Keats's work: I found, as the year wore on, that I had to learn several other poems by him to cover eventualities. These included 'To Autumn', the sonnet 'When I have fears that I may cease to be', 'Ode to a Nightingale', and 'Ode on a Grecian Urn', which took a fair bit of effort. (It took me longer to learn it, probably, than it took Keats to write it.)

People in the street would treat 'Bright Star' with a reverence that was otherwise reserved only for Shakespeare. They would also offer tips on how to perform it. I remember one encounter where I was literally coached in 'Keats projection' by a drama teacher out on the town.

'You need to leave more pauses,' she said. 'Acting is all in the pauses.'

'I see,' I replied. 'OK, how about this.'

I recited.

'Not quite. You need to lean on that "No". The volta. Between the octave and the sestet. Try it again.'

'How's this.'

I recited again.

'Not quite. Try it again. This time...'

The source of this reverence was the tragedy and pity of Keats's death (or a certain film called *Bright Star*), certainly, but also very much the poetry itself, which combines the greatest pitch of emotion with a complex and inexorable movement of thought. 'Bright Star' starts from an image of steadfastness, the star, and journeys through a series of negations to arrive at the poet's own impossible wish for an unchanging love: steadfastness is, finally, unattainable, and the only alternative is death. Keats's poetry is always easy to understand, if you take the trouble. The poetry feels rapturously open. There is no obscurity in it; the poet, it seems, wants you to understand. This is not something one can always say with confidence about the work of other poets.

Keats is one of the great poet-doctors, or physician-writers (Chekhov, William Carlos Williams, Arthur Conan Doyle, W. Somerset Maugham). Why does writing marry so well with doctoring? Doctors see a great deal of life's tragicomedy; they hear many confessions; there must be numerous occasions when they think 'there's a book in this patient'. But these surely cannot be the explanations, since other professions (lawyers, politicians, teachers) also come into intimate contact with people but do not necessarily feel that committing themselves to paper is an equally important activity. My theory is that it is something to do with death, a fact particularly relevant to Keats. Physicians see death regularly. They may be led to wonder: what is this brief thing, human existence? What is it that departs as it is extinguished?

Keats was very familiar with death. Not only did he train as a doctor, but he nursed his brother Tom through the last stages of tuberculosis, and may, in fact, have contracted the disease from him. His brother George also died of it. Poems such as 'La Belle Dame Sans Merci', 'Lamia', and 'The Eve of St Agnes' are suffused with an awareness of the power and omnipresence of death. Keats treated love and death as rival powers. In a letter to Fanny, he wrote: 'I have two luxuries to brood over in my walks...your loveliness, and the hour of my death.' And in another letter:

> I have a sensation at the present moment as though
> I was dissolving... I have been astonished that Men
> could die Martyrs for religion – I have shudder'd at
> it – I shudder no more – I could be martyr'd for my
> Religion – Love is my religion – I could die for that
> – I could die for you.

By 1820 it was clear that he too had contracted tuberculosis, and he decided to sail to Italy for the summer. By the time he arrived in Rome, however, after a disastrous voyage in which the ship was becalmed for long periods, and then put into quarantine as soon as it arrived, he had missed the summer. It was November. He lingered in pain a few more months, dying on the 23rd of February, 1821, aged 25. His physician and friend, Joseph Severn, wrote:

> On the twenty-third, about four, the approaches of death came on. 'Severn – I – lift me up – I am dying – I shall die easy; don't be frightened – be firm, and thank God it has come.' I lifted him up in my arms. The phlegm seemed boiling in his throat, and increased until eleven, when he gradually sank into death, so quiet, that I still thought he slept.

In his short life Keats only practised as a doctor for a couple of months, deciding aged twenty that it was more important to become a writer than continue as a doctor. It was a courageous decision, because it committed him to a life of penury, as well as making his family, who had paid for the training, furious. My feeling is that the decision stemmed from what is omnipresent in his poetry: the sense that life is precious, but short, and that during its brief span our feelings, our sensibilities, must be given primacy. As he said in one letter: 'I am certain of nothing but the holiness of the Heart's affections and the truth of Imagination – What the imagination seizes as Beauty must be truth.'

THE POET: Gerard Manley Hopkins (1844-89) was a Jesuit priest and poetic innovator. Very little of his work was published in his lifetime: the Poet Laureate Robert Bridges championed his work and helped bring it to critical attention after his death.

THE POEM: 'Pied Beauty' was written in 1877. It is a 'curtal sonnet', an invention of Hopkins involving only ten and a half lines as opposed to the conventional fourteen, in which the first stanza is a sestet and the second stanza a quatrain, followed by a half-line. Only two other examples of curtal sonnets by Hopkins exist: 'Peace', and 'Ash Boughs'. It is the best-loved poem by Hopkins, closely followed by 'The Windhover'.

30

Pied Beauty

BY GERARD MANLEY HOPKINS

Glory be to God for dappled things –
    For skies of couple-colour as a brinded cow;
For rose-moles all in stipple upon trout that swim;
    Fresh-firecoal chestnut-falls; finches' wings;
Landscape plotted and pieced – fold, fallow, and plough;
    And áll trádes, their gear and tackle and trim.

All things counter, original, spare, strange;
    Whatever is fickle, freckled, (who knows how?)
With swift, slow; sweet, sour; adazzle, dim;
    He fathers-forth whose beauty is past change:
                      Praise him.

—❧—

This is a 'curtal sonnet', i.e. a sonnet with the end amputated. It is a hymn to both the natural and the man-made world, praising first skies, trout and chestnuts, then fields, ploughs, trades, and the gear and tools of trades (Hopkins liked to watch people working; in that way he was rather like Walt Whitman, and both must have been something of an annoyance as they hovered, scribbling, next to telegraph-pole-erectors and shagreen-casemakers). The poem is about variety, individuality, and changeability, drawing on Hopkins' concept of the unique 'inscape' of each created thing, and yet it ends with a wonderful rhetorical turn: these things all derive from God the Father, who is 'past change'. The end is beautifully, even humorously judged, and in performance it tends to have great emotional impact.

The more I recited it the more I appreciated its extraordinariness. Hopkins' work has no real precedent in the main sequence of English poetry. Almost anything else you care to put your finger on – 'If', 'This Be the Verse', 'The Daffodils', 'Dulce et Decorum Est', and so on – works of genius, to be sure – is explicable in terms of the 'tradition'. Hopkins' work is not.

This is to do with the very strange and personal theories that Hopkins developed about prosody. Conventional metre is organised in feet, adding up to (in the most common case) the five-foot, ten-syllable line of iambic pentameter. Hopkins called this 'running rhythm', and spent his career in undermining it. Instead of writing like Shakespeare, Shelley, Wordsworth or Tennyson, he drew on influences far older, outside the main sequence, such as Anglo-Saxon and Welsh poetry, for which he had to, and did, learn the relevant languages. He called his new style 'sprung rhythm', giving birth to metrical monsters:

> Fresh-firecoal chestnut-falls; finches' wings;
>> Landscape plotted and pieced – fold, fallow, and plough;
> And áll trádes, their gear and tackle and trim.

Here the iamb is abandoned. Hopkins instead throws up

words like brilliant juggling-balls, the liberated feet, eddies of pulse, given unity through hyphenation, alliteration, assonance, and the occasional diacritical mark over important syllables ('áll trádes'). As in another celebrated case ('The Windhover'):

> I caught this morning morning's minion, king-
> dom of daylight's dauphin, dapple-dawn-drawn
> Falcon, in his riding
> Of the rolling level underneath him steady air

... where the phrase 'rolling underneath him steady', with joyous inventiveness, works adjectivally to qualify 'air'.

Christopher Ricks called Hopkins the most original poet of the Victorian age, and it can be argued that he had an important influence on later developments in modernism and free verse. I prefer to see Hopkins as odder than that. As a man and a poet, he was painfully isolated, exiled from his family through his conversion to Catholicism, exiled from his country through his residence in Dublin, and eating his heart out about his religious vocation and the way it might conflict with the business of writing 'secular' verse. These things helped give rise to his originality, but his innovations were not, it seems to me, truly taken up: there is very little of his painstaking rhyming in later Modernist poetry, not much use of his sprung rhythm, which is always deliberate and meticulous (rather against the spirit of free verse), and not much of his Anglo-Saxon attitude towards musical sound-effects such as alliteration and assonance. Hopkins, in art as in life, stands alone.

It was a birthday party in summer: there was a big tent in the garden, and children were running around squealing in grass-stained clothing. The sun covered everything with a lacquer-like sheen. A scent of jasmine hung in the air. The birthday girl was thirty, and had invited all her friends – artists, mainly – to celebrate with her. I had been engaged for the day to mingle among the guests and recite poetry. A highly agreeable job, you might think.

I recited widely: this was a knowledgeable lot. Betjeman got an airing, as did Poe, Robert Graves and (ulp) John Cooper Clarke, who I performed in a Home Counties accent. I was asked to recite Larkin's 'This Be the Verse' several times, and had a go at delivering my own version: 'They feed the ducks, your Mum and Dad... And never go and live in Hull' (see Chapter Two). I was also asked, at the last moment, to deliver a birthday poem, though I had none; but about 30 seconds before the request I had a premonition someone would ask me, and I managed to quasi-improvise a four-line rhyming stanza that, even though it was very dreadful, was slightly better than not saying anything at all. Perhaps best of all, no one said: 'I hate poetry,' 'Get a job,' 'I don't carry change,' 'Do I look like I know anything about poetry?', 'I haven't got any money,' 'Not interested,' or 'Spit some grime.' I could still feel the dislike of poetry, there in the background, moaning like a crated cat, but it was faint.

Then I struck up a conversation with a gentleman standing under a tree and nursing a glass of champagne. He said he was a lecturer in English and American Studies at the University of Sussex, and I vaguely recognised him; I thought I had seen him on a book jacket in my possession. He was a tall man with a head of untamed white hair like an evaporating cirrus cloud. I told him I had been engaged by the hostess to recite poems, and he regarded me with scepticism.

'Which poems?' he asked.

'Any poems you like,' I replied.

'You can recite any poem I mention?'

'Yes,' I said. Of course it was untrue. English poetry is infinite. If its pages were laid breast to breast, they would stretch to Neptune and back.

'Julia,' he said. 'Come and listen to this.'

Julia came over with a friend. They were both very nice middle-class ladies, one in a red dress, one in a green. They were younger than him.

'This man's going to recite a poem for us,' said the lecturer in English and American Studies. 'Whatever we choose. He can recite anything we ask for.'

'Oh, wooonderful,' the green one said. 'I love poetry. Can we have Marvell?'

'No,' said the lecturer in English and American Studies. 'I'm choosing the poem. You can have Marvell later.'

'Marvell is so... marvellous, don't you think?' she said.

A couple more people joined them.

'Yes,' I said. 'I love Marvell.' (I knew a Marvell poem and was eager to forestall the lecturer in English and American Studies.) 'If you want to hear some Marvell, I'd be happy to...'

But the lecturer cut me short. 'What I want you to

recite,' he pronounced slowly, 'is "Pied Beauty" by Gerard Manley Hopkins.'

I felt the most delicious sense of power. I knew I could recite it, and I knew moreover that I could not only recite it, but perform it – which is another thing entirely. It was, in a way, not about me. I could afford the luxury of withdrawing from the occasion. It was about the poem, and the summer afternoon, and the beauty of the natural world as seen through the agonized and ecstatic vision of Father GM Hopkins of the Society of Jesus.

'Very well,' I said. I paused, then began:

Glory be to God for dappled things...

I was 'in the flow'. I had practised the poem many, many times, and for good reason: Hopkins's poetry requires practice. One should not lean too heavily on the 'sprung rhythm', but nevertheless one should acknowledge that it is there. One should slow down when the poem requires it, but not so much as to impede its rolling-on. One should be serious, but one should not start crying.

The poem wound to its conclusion, with its exhortation to worship the Creator, which is difficult, in our godless world, to pitch exactly right; and yet the whole poem depends on one's sincerity, in that moment:

He fathers-forth whose beauty is past change:
                                        Praise him.

I hit the spondee, finished, and bowed. The ladies, hugging

their gins to themselves, clapped. The gins sloshed and sparkled. The lecturer in English and American Studies looked at me with a new respect.

'That,' he said, 'was the second-best rendition of that poem I have ever heard.'

A remark I have been wondering about ever since.

Appendix 1
Give us one of yours

It was very common to be asked for one of my own poems. People assumed I was a poet. This was reasonable. But is any actor ever asked: 'Couldn't we have one of your own plays?' Are art dealers ever asked: 'Can I see one of your own paintings? These paintings here are all well and good. But let's have something from *you.*'

I had written poems, of course, many years before, and I could still remember a couple. But I had long since decided I was no good at it. Now I was being asked for my poems on a regular basis, and what's more, in a tone that sometimes had an edge of hostility. The subtext, I felt, was often: 'What are you doing reciting all this stuff by dead white men? Have some respect for yourself. Be an artist. Be a live white man. Express yourself.'

This is something to do with the myth of the poet, and something to do with the fact that any bloody fool can be a poet, so why shouldn't you (meaning me) be a poet? I write poems, says the punter; why don't you?

So of course I wrote some. An example was 'Four Cats':

Four Cats
I saw, in a dream,
    Four cats
With weeping sores,
    All riding on the backs
Of four horses.

It was a
    Pussy (pus-y)
Pussy
    Posse

Another poem was written in response to conversations about the current poet laureate, Carol Ann Duffy. Duffy is studied widely, appearing on GCSE and A-level syllabi as a Good Thing, and as an inevitable result, no fault of hers, is disliked by some people. I wrote this poem as a comment on the phenomenon:

Carol Duffy
My name is Carol Duffy
    Not forgetting Ann,
My hair is wild and fluffy
    And my poems never scan.

People get all huffy
    Cos they get me in exams,
But they're just being stuffy
    So I couldn't give a damn.

You can see why I gave up.

One trope I would encounter again and again was people asking me to compose a poem *on the spot*, which would have to include a word of their choice: that word had to be worked seamlessly into the poem. At first I was mystified they would expect any human being to be able to do such a thing, but I soon learned that the trope came from a romantic film called *Before Sunrise*, starring Ethan Hawke and Julie Delpy: the pair encounter a sexy hobo who produces poetry on demand, given a single word to start with. Actually, the hobo, once he's got his word, goes and types the poem up on a portable type-writer, taking his time. I was often asked to produce a poem on demand because of this bloody film, and I was never given the luxury of a typewriter. I was even asked by the *Spectator* during an interview for their podcast to work in the word 'Spectator'.

In response to this irritant, I composed a poem in which the word in question could be fitted in without too much sense of incongruity. It was called 'And After All', and existed in two versions, 'And After All 1' and 'And After All 2'. The two 'x's in the poem can be replaced by the word the speaker has asked for, plus a related word or phrase, rhyming, if possible, to give continuity:

And After All 2
And after all
   There are things worth remembering.
There's your mother's whisper in your sulky ear
   On the first morning of your seventh year
There's the quick spring green
   Of the crowns of the queens

Of the forest
  There's x
And x
  But a poem?
The greatest poem is a poor thing.
  It can only make breath speak to breath
And breast to breast
  It can only ring across death
It can only bring forth tears like cheap gin
  And snare the sun
In a thicket of letters.

('Thicket of lettuce?' asked one woman in a beer garden.)

So for example, if the word was 'whiskey', it wouldn't require too great a mental effort to make the middle of the poem read:

  There's a glass of whiskey
    Or three if I'm feeling risky

There were a couple of translations, which I managed in a process of collaboration – for example there was this translation of 'This Be the Verse' by Larkin, by Alex Hubert:

  Ils te niquent, putain, tes vieux.
  Sans faire exprès, mais le font,
  Te lèguent leurs défauts, sérieux,
  T'en ajoutent en plus, c'est con.

Mais ils furent niqués aussi
Par leurs imbéciles anciens,
Niais et sévères par ci
Luttant alors comme des chiens.

Misère dont l'humain hérite
Grossissant comme une tumeur.
Donc quitte les au plus vite
Nique personne, aies de l'honneur.

And the Japanese 'Jabberwocky' aleady given in full above, by
Mimi Dexter:

Buririggu deshita. Suraibi tōbu
　Wēbu de gairu to gimburu shite,
Nante mimuji na borogōbu,
　Mōmu rassu autoguraibimashita ne.

Finally, I learned two poems by my cousin, Russell Dexter,
who died in his early twenties in 1984. Russell, myself and
a couple of other friends met to talk about poetry when we
were in our teens, a time when poetry did seem to be the
most important thing in the world. I often recited these,
and they were often well received. Here's to you, Russell:

The Gauding Gretching Hound
The Gauding, Gretching Hound slouches its way
　Betwixt the twining, tangling vines of rotten oaks.
The screeches on the beeches clear the beeches
　Of bathers because of the screeches

Of the Gauding, Gretching Hound slouching its way
  Betwixt the bloody bodies of bathers
Who bathed too long on the beeches
  Living on human matter, it does not matter how
  but it must be.
The Gauding, Gretching Hound must be.

On the Stage?
That man on the stage, dear,
  Is in an awful rage, dear,
Acting as if he's in a cage, dear.
  The Jaoler's such a sage, dear,
I wonder if they're on the same page, dear?
  This play is taking such an age, dear.
Just look at that man on the stage, dear.

A man once dropped a twenty pound note into my hat for
reciting those two poems one after the other. He had his
arm around a woman and he was in a VERY good mood.

APPENDIX 2
How to remember a poem

1. Choose a good poem in the first place
Good poems – well-crafted ones – tend to be easier to remember. They tend to be about something identifiable, and to have a sense of progression, development, even inevitability. An example might be Shakespeare's sonnet number 130, 'My mistress' eyes are nothing like the sun'. In its fourteen lines it makes an inventory of his mistress's appearance: line one, eyes, line two, lips, line three, breasts, line four, hair, and so on. Of course the poem is more than a roll-call of attributes, but the roll-call facilitates memory. Compare 'High Flight' by John Gillespie Magee, also a sonnet (the one that begins: 'Oh I have slipped the surly bonds of earth/And danced the sky on laughter-silvered wings'). It is also fourteen lines but it's twice as difficult to remember. It's what Orwell might have called a 'good bad poem', full of all sorts of sonorous tropes and poeticizations that have made it popular, but actually rather diffuse, rambling, even contradictory: 'High in the sunlit silence. Hov'ring there/I've chased the shouting wind along.' Well, what is it, silent or shouting? It's also repetitive: 'sun' is mentioned

three times in different contexts, 'high' twice, ('heights' once) 'silent' and 'silence', 'wind' twice, making it all a bit of a mess; one has the strong impression the poet isn't taking much care over his diction.

2. Notice the poet's structures

Rhyme-scheme, certainly. Line length and rhythm, yes. Verse structures, of course. But also more subtle things that you might not notice at first. Balance and contrast, for example. Verses seven, eight and nine of TS Eliot's 'Love Song of J Alfred Prufrock' form a sort of mini-poem in themselves: verse seven begins: 'For I have known them all, already, known them all' and the following two verses ring the changes on this phrase in different ways. Or in 'The Charge of the Light Brigade' by Tennyson, verse three opens: 'Cannon to right of them', which is echoed in verse five, but which develops the phrase differently.

When you memorize a poem, what you are almost doing is writing the poem in reverse: going through all the structural choices the poet has made and pondering on them. When you uncover these choices, there is a sense of insight and connection that naturally reinforces memory.

Structure may often follow meaning. Mary Oliver's free-verse poem 'The Journey' is divided neatly into two halves of eighteen lines each, expressing a 'before' and 'after' the decision to go on the journey: but because there is no line-break you probably wouldn't notice it unless you were looking.

3. Use sequential visualization

You will have heard how people memorize packs of playing cards by associating each card with a character or object, then putting them together to make a story (Mr Bunn the Baker hides in a post-box and leaps out on Mary the Milkmaid, frightening her dog, Pointless the Pug). You can do the same with poems, only more easily, since the images are all there to start with. Take Jenny Joseph's 'Warning': it contains the lines 'I shall sit down on the pavement when I'm tired/And gobble up samples in shops and press alarm bells/And run my stick along the public railings...' This is essentially a list of four items, but because the items are not clearly related as a sequence, they are difficult to remember unless you link them in some way. There are various methods of doing this (see points four and five) but one is sequential visualization. So in this case, you could start by seeing the old lady collapsing onto the pavement in an act of exhausted protest. Why? Because she needs sustenance, food. So she hauls herself to her feet and enters a shop, situated conveniently nearby, where she proceeds to gobble up some samples. Once replete and re-energized, she looks around for a little malevolent fun, and presses an alarm bell. She runs out of the shop cackling, running her stick as she does so along the public railings. The list has now become a little film in which the items unfold in a logical sequence. Now you are more likely a) to remember the list in its entirety and b) not to transpose the items on the list.

4. Notice alliteration and assonance

These are two things that schoolchildren weary of but they are used in every sort of poetry for musical effects, and are very useful for memorizing. They may not be obvious on a first reading, but this fact is an advantage, not a disadvantage. One of the richest feasts of musical effects in English poetry is to be found in 'Look, Stranger' by WH Auden, e.g. in lines 8-11: 'Here by a small field's ending pause/Where the chalk wall falls to the foam and its tall ledges/Oppose the pluck/And knock of the tide.' Alliteration is plentiful: 'Where/wall', 'falls to the foam', 'Oppose the pluck', 'tall/tide'. Assonance can be seen in the clusters 'small/pause/chalk/wall/falls/tall' and 'pluck/knock'. If you personally tease these out, you are more likely to remember them, because you (personally) have made the effort to do so. Afterwards it's possible to piece the poem together in your mind as a series of musical connections.

It doesn't matter, of course, whether the author meant the alliteration or assonance to be there or not.

5. Use initial-letter mnemonics

What do you do about a poem that's apparently unstructured? One tactic is to use initial-letter mnemonics. Ginsberg's 'Howl' doesn't use overt rhyme or regular metre, contains a lot of lists, and is very, very long. How do you remember a line like 'Incomparable blind streets of shuddering cloud and lightning in the mind leaping toward poles of Canada & Paterson, illuminating all the motionless world of Time between'? (And it is only one line.) Well, look at the first three words. 'IBS' are the initial letters. Does that remind you of anything? It does me. That's the thing about mnemonics: they are often very personal, possibly also obscene or scatological. Or irritable. I wouldn't want to say how I remember some poems. The rule is: the sillier and more embarrassing the mnemonic, the better. Let your id take full rein. 'Illuminating all the motionless world of Time between'? Take the significant words in this and it comes out 'I am wtb' What does this mean? You decide. Or take the famous passage from Whitman's 'Song of Myself' that begins: 'In vain the mastodon retreats beneath his own powdered bones...' The significant words in these six lines spell out 'MOO BSE'. Silly, of course, but because silly, difficult to forget.

6. Maintain your memory

There are different depths of memory. It's possible to memorize a sonnet in twenty minutes; the next day the memory may be in tatters. You will need to revise, then re-revise, then re-re-revise, each day. Each time you revise, it will take less time. Finally you won't need to revise every day, but once every two days, then every three, five, seven, ten.

And then you'll be able to say you know the poem by heart.

Appendix 3
Glossary

Alliteration The combination of words with the same first letter so as to create a musical effect. 'Daylight's dauphin, dapple-dawn-drawn falcon' is alliterative. Old English poetry is heavily alliterative, as in 'Piers Plowman' by William Langland: 'In a somer seson, whan softe was the sonne,/I shoop me into shroudes as I a sheep were.'

Anapaest A foot (q.v.) formed of two unstressed syllables followed by a stressed syllable (e.g. 'contradict').

Assonance A poetic strategy whereby similar vowel-sounds are clustered to give a musical effect, as in Auden's 'where the chalk wall falls to the foam...'

Augustan Loosely, eighteenth century English poetry – Pope, Dryden, Johnson.

Caesura A point in the middle of a line where the rhythm seems to stop, before continuing to the end of the line. A device used to break up too-regular or monotonous rhythm. In fact, poets have always sought to break up monotonous chiming effects by the use of 'counterpoint' in metre, in which irregularities are deliberately introduced to give variety. E.g. 'To be or not to be, that is the question.' You'll notice that after the comma (where the caesura is), the iambic rhythm is deliberately disrupted.

Curtal sonnet A sonnet with eleven lines, invented by Gerard Manley Hopkins.

Dactyl A foot (q.v.) formed of a stressed syllable followed by two unstressed syllables (e.g. 'basketball').

Foot A cluster of syllables with a particular stress-pattern. Some types are an iamb (q.v.), a spondee (q.v.) or a molossus (q.v.). The accumulation of feet, usually similar feet, make up the metre (q.v.) of a poem.

Free verse Poetry that has freed itself from traditional rhyme, metre (q.v.) and diction. It's difficult to say when it first originated but its greatest early practitioner in English was probably Walt Whitman in the mid-nineteenth century.

Haiku A Japanese verse form expressing an intensely-felt moment. It often takes the form of just three lines: one five-syllable line, one seven and one five, though in practice, in Japanese, these exact strictures are not necessarily adhered to.

Iamb A metrical foot (q.v.) of two syllables, the second carrying a stress: da-DUM.

Inscape A term invented and used by Gerard Manley Hopkins to describe the unique form, being and beauty of any single object, usually a natural object. It is a theological, rather than a philosophical or biological concept, since the inscape of each object partakes of the holiness of the divine, which lends it its form, being and beauty.

Metaphor A poetic device that involves the identification of one thing with another, rather than the likening of one thing with another (simile). E.g. 'The moon was a gold medallion.' More loosely, a metaphor is anything in a text that refers obliquely to something else. E.g. a toiling sea is a metaphor for the struggle of human life. In poetry, metaphor, by asserting something that is patently not the case – the moon is not a gold medallion – forces us to abandon a rational interpretation of the text, allowing the emotions to dominate our response.

Metre The rhythmic structure of a line, verse or poem. Metre is made up of feet, which have names such as iamb, trochee, spondee, according to the stress-patterns they exhibit. For example, an iamb is da-DUM, a trochee is DA-dum and a spondee is DUM-DUM. 'Shall I compare thee to a summer's day?' is written in five iambs: i.e. da-DUM da-DUM da-DUM da-DUM da-DUM? Because there are five, it's a pentameter, in this case iambic pentameter.

Molossus A foot (q.v.) of three syllables and three stresses (e.g. 'Palm-green shores').

GLOSSARY

Octameter A metre (q.v.) of eight feet (q.v.).

Octave The first eight lines of a sonnet.

Paeon A foot (q.v.) of four syllables consisting of one long syllable and three short syllables, generally with the stress on the first (long) syllable e.g. 'Dirty British'.

Poem 'The best words in the best order' – ST Coleridge. Or, contrapuntally: 'Everything is shit, except poetry.' – Roberto Bolano.

Poetaster A laughably preening and untalented poet.

Prosody The study of metre (q.v.) in poetry. Topics of discussion might include the caesura (q.v.), feet (q.v.), vowel-length, vowel and consonantal relationships, etc.

Quatrain A four-line verse.

Rhyme-scheme The succession of rhymes in a poem. A rhyme-scheme can be represented in shorthand by allotting letters to individual new rhymes as they crop up; so the rhyme-scheme of Larkin's 'This Be the Verse' is ABAB CDCD EFEF.

Scansion The degree to which a line of poetry conforms to a pre-set metre. If the scansion is incompetent, we can say that the line 'doesn't scan'. However, most competent poets deliberately introduce irregularities into scansion to break up the monotony. So the rule is: know the rules before you break the rules.

Sestet The last six lines of a sonnet.

Sonnet A verse-form of fourteen lines, usually written in iambic pentameter. Petrarchan sonnets rhyme ABBA ABBA CDE CDE or ABBA ABBA CDC DCD; Shakespearean sonnets rhyme ABAB CDCD EFEF GG, where each letter stands for a particular rhyming sound.

Spondee A metrical foot (q.v.) of two syllables, both equally stressed: DUM-DUM. Often used at the end of a line.

Sprung rhythm A type of metre (q.v.) pioneered by Gerard Manley Hopkins, influenced by Anglo-Saxon poetry. In sprung rhythm, syllables can form irregular clusters. Hopkins sometimes used diacritical marks on the tops of letters to indicate where stresses should fall, but in many places did not, meaning that sprung rhythm is a matter of interpretation.

Stanza Another name for a verse (1).

Tetrameter A metre (q.v.) of four feet (q.v.)

Trochee A metrical foot (q.v.) of two syllables, the first carrying a stress: DA-dum.

Verse (1) An arrangement of lines to form a unit, after

which there is a line space, and a new verse may begin. A poetic paragraph.

Verse (2) Another word for poetry, as in 'deathless verse'.

Villanelle A verse form made up of five stanzas of three lines each and one final stanza of four, with two lines that repeat alternately and are joined in the final couplet. Many poets have enjoyed playing with villanelles, among them Wendy Cope, Elizabeth Bishop and WH Auden.

Volta Literally 'turn'. It refers to the moment in a poem in which the flow of thought or emotion abruptly changes.

'Poets are the
unacknowledged legislators
of the world'
Percy Bysshe Shelley